Outlook 2007

DISCARD

Receive a $10 rebate on this book!

Visit www.apress.com/promo for rebate details and form.

ISBN-13: 978-1-59059-796-5
ISBN-10: 1-59059-796-6

Outlook 2007

BEYOND
THE MANUAL

Tony Campbell, Jonathan Hassell

Apress®

Outlook 2007: Beyond the Manual
Copyright © 2007 by Tony Campbell

ISBN-13 (pbk): 978-1-59059-796-5

ISBN-10 (pbk): 1-59059-796-6

Printed and bound in the United States of America 9 8 7 6 5 4 3 2 1

Distributed to the book trade worldwide by Springer-Verlag New York, Inc., 233 Spring Street, 6th Floor, New York, NY 10013. Phone 1-800-SPRINGER, fax 201-348-4505, e-mail orders-ny@springer-sbm.com, or visit http://www.springeronline.com.

For information on translations, please contact Apress directly at 2560 Ninth Street, Suite 219, Berkeley, CA 94710. Phone 510-549-5930, fax 510-549-5939, e-mail info@apress.com, or visit http://www.apress.com.

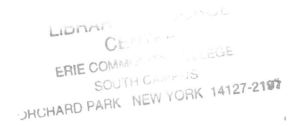

This book is dedicated to my wife, Sharon. Love you, babe.
—Tony

To my wife, Lisa. Thanks for everything. Oh, and thanks to the cats and dog for keeping things interesting.
—Jon

Contents at a Glance

Contents

CHAPTER 6

Notes and Journals 91

CHAPTER 7

Task Management 105

About the Authors

TONY CAMPBELL is an experienced Microsoft consultant specializing in the architecture and design of secure, Microsoft-centric business solutions. He also has vast experience in many other industry niches such as networking, collaboration, security, business logic, and disaster recovery and resilience. Tony has been involved with all sizes of businesses, from the very small to the very large, and has successfully delivered secure, reliable, robust solutions to more than 150,000 clients in his 18 years in the business. Tony started his career back in the 80s as a "green-screen" mainframe programmer for the British Meteorological Office, finally arriving after a long journey in his current role as a self-employed IT consultant and author.

Tony is a regular contributor to a variety of journals distributed across the globe and has been involved in the production of software manuals, user guides, white papers, hardware manuals, and training courses for many of his clients in the past decade. His love of writing has led to the publication of his fiction in a variety of small presses and magazines.

JONATHAN HASSELL is an author, consultant, and speaker on a variety of IT topics. His published works include *RADIUS* (O'Reilly, 2002), *Hardening Windows, Second Edition* (Apress, 2005), *Using Microsoft Windows Small Business Server 2003* (Apress, 2006), and *Learning Windows Server 2003* (O'Reilly, 2006). His work appears regularly in such periodicals as *Windows IT Pro* magazine, *PC Pro*, and *TechNet Magazine*. He also speaks worldwide on topics ranging from networking and security to Windows administration. He is currently an editor at Apress.

Acknowledgments

This was by far the toughest book I've ever written simply because of extremely tight deadlines when turning around editorial and production reviews. Without the dedication of the entire team at Apress, I don't think this book would have been ready in even twice the time it took to pull it together. So, for that reason, I would like to sincerely thank (and offer free beer to anyone who accepts) the team at Apress that made this book happen. Well done, all of you; it has been a pleasure to work (for even such a small amount of time) with such a dedicated and friendly, and yet highly persuasive, bunch.

Tony Campbell

Introduction

As Microsoft Office users and dedicated enthusiasts since the early days of Office 95, both Jon and I have been astonished by the amount of functionality that resides within Outlook—functionality that is largely ignored by the majority of users.

Don't get me wrong: this lack of understanding is through no fault of you guys; instead, it's due to Outlook being so much richer in capabilities than the simple messaging client it's purported to be by many business users. When someone says "email," people think of Outlook, but when someone says "workflow, calendaring, task management, to-do lists, RSS feed reading, and blog authoring," Outlook is less often at the top of their thoughts. More often than not, when Outlook is deployed in business, it's rarely sold as anything but a corporate email client.

Rarely do companies fully embrace Outlook for what it really is, and more important, it's extremely rare for users to receive any kind of guidance or training on the underlying power that this important productivity tool contains. So, that's why we wrote this book: to empower Outlook users with the knowledge they need to totally overhaul how they conduct their day-to-day business.

Outlook 2007 is the most comprehensive messaging and organizational tool on the market, and with this latest release, Outlook incorporates a whole bunch of new and exciting updates that will take you into the next major Internet revolution, such as the RSS feed reader/authoring capability for reading and publishing directly to blogs and a much simplified approach to organization, collaboration, and interoperability with server-side solutions such as SharePoint.

We have written *Outlook 2007: Beyond the Manual* as a one-stop-shop learning tool to explain exactly how the experts use Outlook 2007; it will take you further and faster into the depths of lesser used and lesser understood functionality and will allow you to start digitally managing your own time and work more effectively.

Who This Book Is For

Outlook 2007: Beyond the Manual is a guide for anyone who wants to get more from the software installed on their desktop. If you are currently an Outlook user and want to learn more about this sophisticated product's extended set of capabilities, this book is definitely for you. Alternatively, if you are not currently using Outlook (at home or in the office) and are in a position where you might be wondering whether to purchase it, or if you are wondering how to convince the IT department that Outlook makes good business sense, this book is certainly going to help you with the justification. Administrators, business analysts, power users, CEOs, and home users will all reap huge and immediate rewards from a better understanding of what Outlook 2007 can do.

Using this book, you will immediately see the benefits of what Outlook 2007 can bring to both your home life and your work life, and these benefits, with just a little practice, will offer not only personal and organizational benefits but will also increase productivity and lead to considerable savings in both money and time.

The only preconception this book makes of you is that you are familiar with the basics of email and electronic diaries; the rest, you'll learn in due course.

How This Book Is Structured

Outlook 2007: Beyond the Manual is divided into thirteen functionally specific chapters, with each covering a unique aspect of the technology that needs exposing. To give you a feel for what's to come, here is a chapter-by-chapter summary of the book you are about to read.

Chapter 1, "What's New and What's Improved in Outlook 2007"

Chapter 1 takes a look at the new features available in Outlook 2007 as well as taking a short walk through the basics of setting up and using email. We also cover the basic system requirements for installing Outlook 2007; then, at the end of this chapter, you'll find a comprehensive list of keyboard shortcuts that will help speed up your navigation around the interface.

Chapter 2, "Messaging"

Being able to send and receive email is without question the core function of Outlook, so this chapter covers some of the ancillary capabilities Outlook provides for enhancing this messaging capability. It covers using message templates to make sending messages more versatile, setting expiration dates to allow you to expire email content at a given time, using the Out Of Office Assistant, and integrating Outlook with Windows Live Messenger.

Chapter 3, "Message Organization"

Following on from the previous chapter, this chapter focuses on organizing email using features such as search folders to create query-based folders that are virtual representations of email in your inbox. We also cover rule and junk mail filtering as an introduction to using send and receive groups to split how individual accounts collect and process email.

Chapter 4, "Contacts and Address Books"

The goal of this chapter is to explain how you can best use Outlook's inherent ability to act as your personal address book. It looks at creating and using contact items and then elaborates on how contacts are stored in address books. The way you organize your contacts and address books in Outlook has much bearing on the net benefit you get out from the product.

Chapter 5, "Calendaring"

The calendar capability has been around for many, many versions of Outlook, but in Outlook 2007 it has been upgraded significantly, making it much more useful than before. This is largely due to the integration of color categories and its much improved interface; however, the new searching and sharing features make this so much more than simply somewhere to jot down future events—at last it's a fully featured personal information management tool.

Chapter 6, "Notes and Journals"

This chapter delves into some of the extra features Outlook provides. Specifically, you can use the notes capability to quickly jot down information (when you're on the phone, for example) and then further process that information into a more manageable format, such as an email, a task, or an appointment. The Journal is one of the least used yet most useful features in Outlook; it gives you an extremely versatile auditing capability, where you can have Outlook log the time you spend on tasks and record emails you send to specified recipients. There is also a manual method for entering Journal entries that cannot be recorded automatically, whereby you can also assign time in the audit log to phone calls, meetings, and ad hoc discussions.

Chapter 7, "Task Management"

Chapter 7 is devoted to managing tasks. In previous versions of Outlook, task management was poor, but Microsoft has really excelled in uplifting the experience in Outlook 2007, introducing the all-new To-Do Bar as a way of instantly seeing what you have to do and when. This chapter also covers how SharePoint task lists can be integrated into Outlook, bridging the gap that once existed between client and server technologies.

Chapter 8, "Storage Management"

This chapter covers managing Outlook storage, focusing on the underlying data files that are used to contain Outlook items associated with each of your accounts. You'll learn about online and offline storage and how you can use these differing methods to work remotely from your ISP or email server.

Chapter 9, "Color Categories"

This chapter dives into color categories (Outlook 2007's evolution of the previous version's unwieldy attempt at categorizing items) by introducing you to this much improved method for visually assessing email messages, tasks, and appointments that are related to each other. Color categories are one of the most important developments in Outlook 2007 that help you organize and process information more effectively and form the foundation for much of the text covered later in the book.

Chapter 10, "Customization"

The strength of Outlook comes from its ability to be adapted to suit your needs as those needs change. Chapter 10 looks at how you can customize standard Outlook functionality using profiles, command-line switches, views, and the Outlook Today web interface to shape it into a bespoke tool that services your every whim.

Chapter 11, "Security and Backup"

These days, no IT book would be complete without covering security. Because Outlook 2007 is so immensely feature rich and capable of managing your every need, it stands to reason that the underlying application is extensive. So, what has Microsoft done to ensure all this private and personal data is protected? This chapter covers all you need to know about securing Outlook; it specifically covers certificates, macro security, add-ins, and privacy, which are all managed through the all-new management console called the Trust Center.

Chapter 12, "Outlook Outside the Office (or Home)"

More and more of us are becoming mobile or home-based workers these days. This chapter looks at the best ways of configuring Outlook when you have no real fixed abode or you are on the move. Outlook 2007 provides several features and services for mobile workers that allow you to access email over any kind of connectivity, be it dial-up, LAN, or Internet.

Chapter 13, "Forms and Macros"

Building on what you learned in Chapter 10, Chapter 13 goes further into customizing Outlook using forms and macros. This chapter looks at the basic principles of both technologies and then takes you through a working example of creating and publishing a basic form with an embedded Excel spreadsheet control. A short introduction to macros is also included to whet your appetite.

Prerequisites

If you will be installing Outlook 2007 on Windows XP, ensure you have previously upgraded to Service Pack 2 and downloaded and installed the Windows Desktop Search version 3.0 or later in order to get the most out of your new software.

Contacting the Authors

Tony Campbell is the managing director of his own consultancy company, Procyon Services, specializing in designing and delivering secure Microsoft server-based solutions for small, medium, and large businesses. Tony also provides authoring services to his clients for producing manuals, training material, guide books, and white papers on a wide variety of subjects. If you have any questions about this book or about Outlook 2007 in general, please feel free to email him at the following address, or drop him a message through his website. Like you, Tony is an extremely busy guy and might not be able to get back to you immediately, so please be patient.

Website address: http://www.procyon-services.co.uk

Email address: tony.campbell@procyon-services.co.uk

Jon is also a pretty busy guy, with speaking, travel, editing, and writing, but he'd love to hear from you when you get a chance. Email him at:

contact@scribnertechmediacorp.com.

CHAPTER 1

What's New and What's Improved in Outlook 2007

U nlike its counterparts in the Office suite, Outlook 2007 isn't just a single-purposed tool like, for example, Microsoft Word or Microsoft Excel; instead, it is a conglomeration of functionality designed to help you manage all aspects of your daily life.

This chapter provides the following information:

- An introduction to Outlook 2007
- A look at the new features included in this version of the product
- The system requirements for installing Outlook 2007
- A tour around the new interface
- How to subscribe to RSS feeds
- How to set up your POP3 account with an ISP
- How to send and receive email using Outlook 2007
- A list of the most commonly used keyboard shortcuts

Aside from the obvious function of acting as your email client and connecting to an Internet service provider (ISP) or corporate Exchange Server machine, Outlook can assist in managing and making sense of large quantities of information (of which we all have an increasing amount) using a clever color categorization system. With these color categories, it's possible to visually assess large quantities of information in your inbox for items that have a common theme, saving you time and ultimately money. The enhanced calendaring facility allows you to better organize your daily schedules, set up meetings with colleagues (online or offline), and keep tabs on where your team is, as well as synchronize easily with portable devices so you can take your information and schedule with you when you're on the move. Outlook 2007 improves on previous versions of the calendar by making sharing items much easier both on a local scale and across the Internet through Office Online.

So, what exactly can Outlook do for you? The following list summarizes the main capabilities Outlook brings to your desktop:

• Record contact information in a digital address book, where you can store dozens of pieces of information (including photographs) about your contacts, as shown in Figure 1-1.

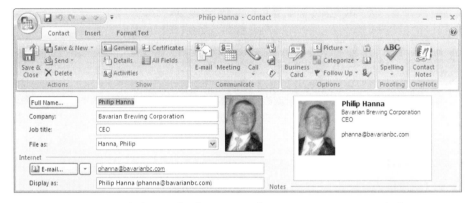

Figure 1-1. Store a plethora of information about your contacts, including a digital photograph.

• Manage your time using the calendaring feature, which allows you to book meetings, invite others to collaborate with you, and see at a glance where you are supposed to be over the course of a day, week, or month.

• Schedule your work with the comprehensive task management system, which allows you to instantly assign tasks to your schedule from emails, from calendar items, or from simple Outlook notes. Task tracking using the new To-Do Bar shown in Figure 1-2 allows you to instantly prioritize your day's work and streamline the way you operate.

• Record instantly your thoughts using Outlook notes, whereby small snippets of information are recorded in free form that can later become the basis of tasks, email, or calendar appointments.

• Send and receive emails either through your corporate email system or through an ISP via the Internet.

Figure 1-2. The To-Do Bar makes information immediately available on the desktop.

What's New in Outlook 2007

The three most striking new features that have arrived with Outlook 2007 are instant search, the To-Do Bar, and attachment previewing. Aside from these new features, you'll also see many improvements in the features you've come to recognize as part of Outlook. Color categories, for example, replace the old Master Category List with a much simplified yet highly effective color-coding system for grouping any related items within your information store.

Instant search is an extremely fast way of searching through your inbox; a simple search string starts building up the results of your query as soon as you start to type. Instant search leverages the underlying Windows Desktop Search technology built into Windows Vista; if you are a Windows XP user, you can download the Windows Desktop Search add-in from http://www.microsoft.com/windows/desktopsearch.

The To-Do Bar offers you an immediate view of your day's activities, displaying your calendar, task list, and any up-and-coming appointments you might have scheduled. By default, the To-Do Bar is on the right side of the main Outlook screen, and it gives you access to this information at all times when you are using Outlook. This saves you from having to switch to the Calendar view or Task view to see what's coming up.

The attachment previewer is probably one of the least publicized yet most powerful features included in this version of Outlook. By using the attachment previewer, you can click a message attachment within the Preview pane, and then, as long as there is an attachment previewer installed for that file type (more and more are being developed all the time), you will see the attachment inside the Preview pane without having to separately open it. Also, if you receive an email message that has another email message as an attachment, by clicking the attachment you will immediately see the content in the Preview pane. This all happens within the bounds of the single Preview pane without cluttering up your desktop while each attachment is opened separately. Another great feature of using the attachment previewer is that some of the more insidious content types, such as scripts, macros, and ActiveX, will not work. To use scripts and code, you will need to use the parent application that created the attachment where you can have greater control over what that content might be able to do.

> **NOTE** By default, Outlook provides preview support for the entire Office suite of applications, meaning you can preview files created in Word, Power-Point, Excel, and Visio. Third-party developers will also be developing previewers for their own products, and these will be available on Microsoft's website. If you try to preview an attachment that does not have a previewer installed—for example, if you try to view a PDF document—Outlook will prompt you to go online, where you can browse to see whether one is available. If you click Browse for Previewers Online, Internet Explorer fires up and automatically instigates a search for that file type's previewer.

Another great enhancement to functionality is the upgraded integration of follow-up flags with the To-Do Bar. Anything you flag for follow-up will immediately appear in the To-Do Bar task list, henceforth remaining apparent on the desktop until you remove the flag. The To-Do Bar task list also contains tasks you have specifically created as part of your daily work profile (ones to which you have assigned a particular start and end date). This consolidation helps you store different types of information as tasks (some come as email and some come from meetings) but lets you treat them all with the same level of importance.

Much greater integration of Outlook 2007 with server solutions allow, for example, Exchange Server to assist you better in meeting planning, such as by offering the best time for all required attendees to attend a meeting; in addition, SharePoint Server can synchronize team calendars, task lists, and discussion boards to allow your personal desktop system to be leveraged as a collaborative tool within the context of a SharePoint site.

Really Simple Syndication (RSS) feeds are becoming more widespread with the increasing popularity of blogging; these feeds are XML-based web pages that are updated when a new blog post is submitted to a site. An RSS feed reader will parse the XML on each of the websites you subscribe to and make available all the latest posts. Outlook leverages this RSS technology, allowing you to subscribe to RSS feeds through the Navigation Pane. We cover subscribing to an RSS feed later in this chapter.

In addition, the calendar has been improved significantly to help you better share and collaborate with others. It's possible to send a snapshot of your calendar to co-workers, who can then view it using a web browser. If you prefer to share a calendar with remote users, you can subscribe to an Internet calendar service and synchronize appointments to a central Internet server. Anyone with Internet access can be authorized to participate.

> **NOTE** Microsoft provides its own Internet calendar service on Office Online. For more details of the services available, take a look at `http://office.microsoft.com`. You will need to create a Windows Live ID account in order to use the Office Online services.

The security enhancements in Outlook 2007 make it undoubtedly the most robust and threat-resistant email client on the market. Using the new Trust Center (a centralized interface for managing security settings), you can easily manage your macros, privacy settings, Outlook add-ins, and attachments.

Outlook also includes an update to the junk email filter, which makes sorting out unwanted emails much more reliable than before, and a new digital postmarking feature, which provides a digital stamp on all emails created in Outlook 2007 that marks them as legitimate before being sent. This postmark exploits the fact that spammers send bulk email programmatically from an email client; if they tried to do this using Outlook 2007, their computer would be so significantly slowed down because of the vast number of digital postmarks it had to generate that the spammer would be put out of business. If an Outlook 2007 client receives an email with an attached postmark, it can be assumed the message originated from someone who is not a spammer, so it can be automatically delivered to the inbox rather than the junk email folder.

Finally, look out for Outlook gadgets available to plug into your Windows Vista Sidebar. These fantastic, yet really simple, add-ins for Vista allow you to have To-Do Bar–style functionality available on your desktop even when Outlook is minimized. To get Outlook gadgets for Vista, visit `http://gallery.microsoft.com`.

Outlook System Requirements

Outlook 2007 might come as part of the Microsoft Office suite, but it has its own publicized set of system requirements pertinent to running its myriad features. Table 1-1 shows the minimum requirements laid out by Microsoft for running

Outlook 2007; you should consider these requirements the minimum requirements and not the requirements for Outlook running at peak performance. A better processor and more memory will always act to your advantage.

Table 1-1. Minimum Hardware and Software Requirements for Running Outlook 2007

System Component	Minimum Requirement
CPU	500MHz
Memory	256MB (more like 1GB if you are running Vista)
Hard disk	1.5GB
Optical drive	CD-ROM
Display	1024×768-resolution monitor
Operating system	Windows XP with Service Pack 2 and Windows Desktop Search 3.0
Browser	Internet Explorer 6.0

Exploring the New Interface

In truth, the new interface for Outlook 2007 is not significantly different from that of Outlook 2003, especially when you consider the vastly different approach taken in other products such as Word 2007 with the new Ribbon. However, the layout of the interface has changed a little, and you should note a few additions before you start using Outlook.

First, positioned on the right side of the screen is the To-Do Bar. You can switch it, using the View menu, to Normal, Minimized, or Off, and you can configure exactly how much information appears on the screen. You can also minimize or display the To-Do Bar using the chevrons at the top of the window. These chevrons also appear on the Navigation Pane on the left side of the screen and do a similar job, minimizing or displaying it as required.

Second, instant search is available in the main Outlook window next to the currently selected folder name. You can simply start typing your query in this text entry field to obtain a set of results. The search results will appear in the main window, and the folder name is augmented with *(Search Results)*.

Next, the calendar looks a lot nicer than before (although this is subtle) and, more important, gives you immediate access to tasks at the bottom of the screen, as shown in Figure 1-3.

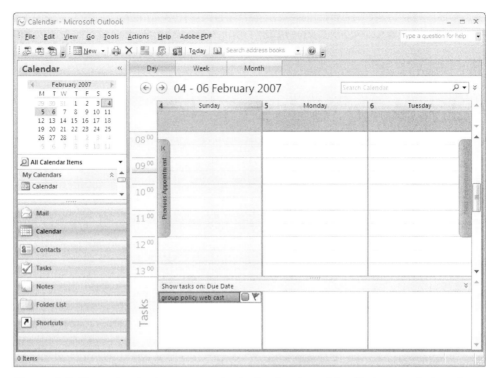

Figure 1-3. The calendar is more aesthetically pleasing with a Tasks pane below the main window.

You'll notice when you try to compose a new email that you are using Word as your editor. The features of Outlook have been represented on the Word Ribbon bar, as shown in Figure 1-4, so you will use the Ribbon as you would if you were writing a document in Word, but you now have immediate access to business cards, attachments, digital signatures, and your address book.

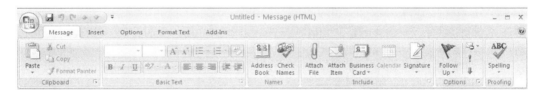

Figure 1-4. The Word Ribbon is used when you create a new message.

With the introduction of Business Card view for contacts, you get yet another way of displaying information about your colleagues, friends, and associates. However, this is a big improvement since the way the information is exposed looks very much like physical business cards, with space for a digital image. This allows you to add a photograph of the contact or maybe a digital image of the contact's corporate logo.

The Tasks interface has also had a makeover, augmented now with the facility to manage your to-do list. This information is immediately transferred to the To-Do Bar to make it available at all times.

Subscribing to RSS Feeds

RSS feeds are a way for content publishers (such as bloggers) to push their information to your system through a simple subscription mechanism. This allows you to automatically receive updates when they are made available on the associated website. Content provided by RSS feeds is typically free, and subscribing to a feed using the feed reader built into Outlook is easy.

Websites that provide RSS feeds usually have an orange RSS symbol somewhere on the page that denotes the fact that you can subscribe.

To get started, you'll need to copy the link to the RSS content from the target website by selecting the RSS symbol (in Internet Explorer) and then copying this URL to the Clipboard. Now, go to Outlook, select Mail, right-click RSS Feeds in the Navigation Pane, and then select Add a New RSS Feed. In the New RSS Feed dialog box, paste the link to the RSS URL into the text entry box, and then click Add. You will see a warning that says you should subscribe only to content you trust and that asks whether you really want to proceed. If you are sure, click Yes.

From now on, as your system synchronizes using send/receive, new posts are downloaded and made available under the specific feed's name in the Navigation Pane.

A few good RSS feeds to get you going are as follows:

- Gain access to Microsoft's Office Online demonstrations, training material, and online quizzes at `http://office.microsoft.com/download/file.aspx?assetid=HX101648651033`.

- Get up-to-the-minute news of what Apress is publishing at `http://www.apress.com/rss/whatsnew.xml`.

- See what's happening in the world with the top-ten news stories coming from MSNBC news at `http://rss.msnbc.msn.com/id/3032091/device/rss/rss.xml`.

- Read all about Windows Vista on our very own blog at `http://feeds.feedburner.com/VistaBeyondTheManual`.

- Find out what developments are happening in Microsoft regarding Office Online at the team blog at `http://blogs.msdn.com/inside_office_online/rss.aspx`.

NOTE You may have noticed when you add a new feed that there is an option to import something called an OPML file. This Outline Processor Markup Language (OPML) file describes the underlying XML data used to create information (such as the blogs) and forms the basis of the feeds to which you subscribe. Some sites may provide their syndication using the RSS technique, some may provide OPML directly, and some provide both. RSS is more commonly used today as the method of subscribing, but some OPML sites still exist.

Setting Up a POP3 Account

This section explains how to set up your POP3 account access. The Account Settings dialog box has changed somewhat from Outlook 2003, so it's worth running through this just to make sure you can get access to your ISP:

1. Select Tools ➤ Account Settings. This will open the Account Settings dialog box shown in Figure 1-5.

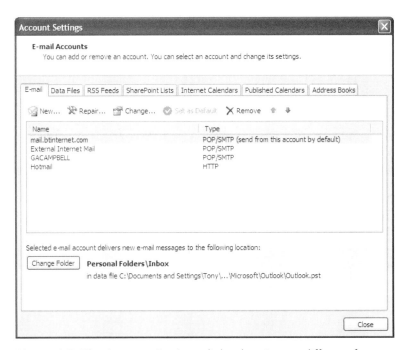

Figure 1-5. The Account Settings dialog box is very different from previous versions of Outlook.

2. Select the E-mail tab, and then click New. This starts the Add New E-mail Account Wizard and displays the page shown in Figure 1-6. From here, select the topmost option (Microsoft Exchange, POP3, IMAP, or HTTP), and then click Next.

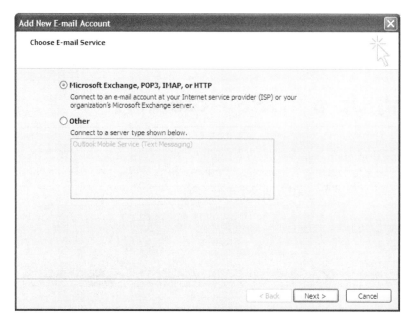

Figure 1-6. Run through the Add New E-mail Account Wizard to set up your ISP account.

3. On the Auto Account Setup page, you have two options. You can have Outlook try to automatically configure your account using your name, email address, and password. If your ISP permits this, your email address is the same as your email domain name, and you log in using your email address as your username; then click Next. If this does not work or you prefer to set up the connection manually, select the checkbox at the bottom of the screen, Manually Configure Server Settings or Additional Server Types. You don't have to fill in the details on this screen if you choose to configure this manually. When you're done, click Next.

4. If you are configuring the connection manually, select the appropriate email service on the Choose E-mail Service page shown in Figure 1-7. In the case of your setting up a POP3 service, select the topmost choice, Internet E-mail, and then click Next.

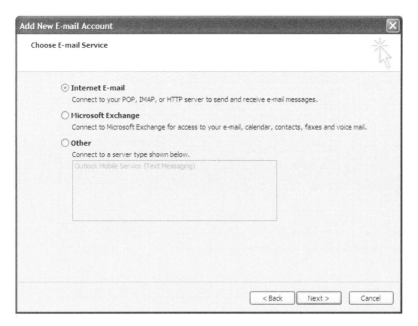

Figure 1-7. Select Internet E-mail to set up a POP3 account.

5. You are now required to enter the information specific for your ISP account, such as server names, username, password, and email address. This screen should be familiar to anyone who has used previous versions of Outlook, as shown in Figure 1-8.

6. Check whether you have entered the details correctly by clicking Test Account Settings. This will attempt to log in to your server and send a test message using the account details you have specified. If there is a problem, you'll see a warning message suggesting that the test failed. If this is the case, double-check the details you have entered, and then check with your ISP to see whether any additional requirements for connecting are required.

7. When you're done, click Next. When you see the Congratulations page, click Finish. You are now ready to start sending and receiving emails on the Internet.

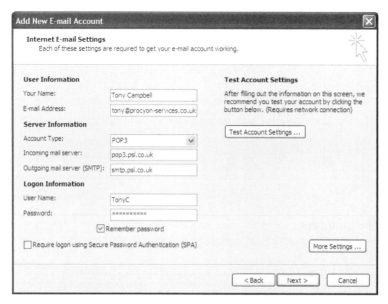

Figure 1-8. Enter the details supplied by your ISP, and then click Test Account Settings.

In some cases, ISPs use additional security settings or have specific network port requirements for providing the connection. If you are required to configure additional settings, you can access these by clicking More Settings and then selecting the Outgoing Server tab, as shown in Figure 1-9.

Figure 1-9. Configure server security settings particular to your ISP's requirements.

You can also configure how you'd like Outlook to handle messages stored on a remote server. The default action is to pull the message down to your computer and delete it from the server, but if you click the Advanced tab on the Settings dialog box, as shown in Figure 1-10, you can ask Outlook to leave a copy of the message on the server for a set period of time before it is removed. In this way, you have time to pull your messages down to any number of clients you require.

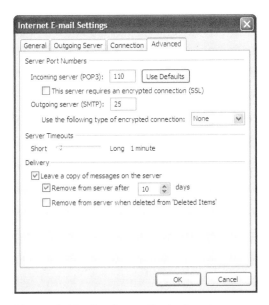

Figure 1-10. Configure Outlook to leave a copy of your messages on the server for a set period of time.

Sending, Receiving, and Responding to Email

For any readers new to Outlook, we should probably go through the basics of composing and sending email. The following is a whistle-stop tour of basic functionality, and we will delve a lot deeper into this functionality throughout the course of the rest of this book.

Sending an email is probably one of the easiest and most useful tasks you can perform with Outlook—and probably the task most widely associated with it. Once you have an account configured with an ISP, you have to take a few quick steps to getting your message on its way. The following steps will allow you to compose and send an email to whomever you choose, making sure you understand the basics:

1. To compose a new email, locate the New button on the toolbar, click the drop-down arrow next to it, and then select Mail Message from the menu. You will immediately see a new, blank email message, with Untitled – Message in the title bar.

2. In the To field, you can type the email address of your intended recipient, or if you have already stored some email addresses in your address book, click the To button to see this list.

3. You can add multiple recipients to the To list by separating each one with a semicolon. You can also add courtesy copy (CC) recipients to the message in the CC field.

4. Add a subject heading to the email to identify what the email is about to the recipient. This is becoming more important these days because spam filters look for specific blueprints that identify spam, one of which is a message with a blank subject line.

5. Now you can type your message using all the rich formatting available in Word to make your message look as professional as possible.

6. If you want to add attachments (documents, pictures, spreadsheets, and so on), click Insert view on the Ribbon menu, and then click the required button designating the type of attachment you need to send to the recipient, such as Attach File or Picture.

7. Click Options view to request a read or deliver receipt, thus sending you an acknowledgment when the recipient receives and looks at the email.

8. Use Format Text view to modify how the text in the message looks. This menu looks much the same as the standard text-formatting menu in Word.

9. Back in Message view, you can select the account you want to send your email from using the Account button (if you have more than one account configured, that is); then when you are ready, you can click Send to send it on its way. In the example shown in Figure 1-11, notice that there are four separate accounts configured here, the default being the one at the top.

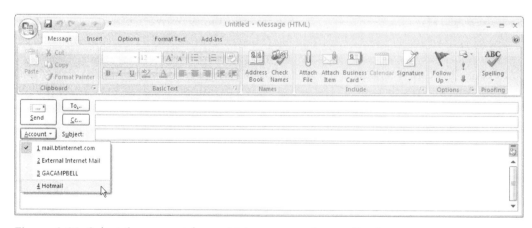

Figure 1-11. Select the account from which you want the email to be sent.

So, what happens when you receive an email? New emails appear in your inbox, displayed in bold text format until you read them. To open an email, simply double-click it, and it will open in its own window. You can also see the contents of an email in the Reading pane (by default this is on the right side of the screen, but you can adjust it). If you look beneath your Inbox folder in the Navigation Pane on the left side of the screen, you'll see the Junk E-Mail folder where Outlook's junk e-mail filter will dispose of emails it deems to be spam. You can look in here for email that might have been mistakenly dumped as spam; right-click it, select Junk E-Mail, and then choose Add Sender to Safe Senders List. This will ensure that the junk e-mail filter will not mistake email from this sender in the future as spam.

When you have finished reading an email, you have the option of replying to the sender or forwarding the message to someone else. You can easily carry out these actions. Just hit the appropriate button for Reply, Reply to All, or Forward.

> **CAUTION** Reply to All sends your reply to everyone listed in the To and CC fields of the original message. Be careful that you don't reply to a vast number of recipients accidentally; system administrators can become somewhat agitated when corporate announcements suddenly generate a large quantity of unwanted chatter on their networks.

Using Keyboard Shortcuts

As with practically every Windows product, Outlook 2007 has its own set of keyboard shortcuts that speed up working with the interface. Granted, these take a little getting used to but, once mastered, will undoubtedly be your most efficient way of navigating and working with Outlook features. The following tables, Tables 1-2 through 1-9, show a comprehensive list of all the keyboard shortcuts available in Outlook 2007.

> **NOTE** When composing text in Outlook, you actually use the underlying features of Word to provide the formatting. For this reason, the standard keyboard shortcuts in Word are also available through the Outlook interface; for example, Ctrl+B will provide bold text, and Ctrl+I will toggle italics.

Table 1-2. Keyboard Shortcuts Available in Outlook 2007 for Standard User Interface Navigation

Action	Shortcut
Mail	Ctrl+1
Calendar	Ctrl+2
Contacts	Ctrl+3
Tasks	Ctrl+4
Notes	Ctrl+5
Folder list	Ctrl+6
Shortcuts	Ctrl+7
Next message (with a message open)	Ctrl+. (period)
Previous message (with a message open)	Ctrl+, (comma)
Move between Navigation Pane, Outlook main windows, and Reading pane	F6
Move around Navigation Pane	Arrow keys
Change folder	Ctrl+Y
Go to Search	F3
In the Reading pane, previous message	Ctrl+, (comma)
In the Reading pane, page down through text	Spacebar
In the Reading pane, page up through text	Shift+spacebar
Expand or collapse group in Navigation Pane	Shift++ (plus sign) or Shift+– (minus sign)
Expand or collapse group in inbox	Left arrow or right arrow
Next field in Reading pane	Shift+Tab
Previous field in Reading pane	Ctrl+Tab
Previous view in main Outlook window	Alt+B
Forward to next view in Outlook window	Alt+right arrow
Start a send/receive for all defined send/receive groups	F9
Start a send/receive for the current folder	Shift+F9
Define send/receive groups	Ctrl+Alt+S
Play a macro	Alt+F8
Select the InfoBar and show the menu of commands	Ctrl+Shift+W

Table 1-3. Keyboard Shortcuts Pertaining to Search

Action	Shortcut
Find a message or other such item	Ctrl+E
Clear the search box	Esc
Expand search to include all mail, calendar, or contact items depending on module	Ctrl+Alt+A
Expand the search query builder	Ctrl+Alt+W
Use advanced find	Ctrl+Shift+F
Create a new search folder	Ctrl+Shift+P
Search for text within an item	F4
Find next match within item	Shift+F4
Find and replace	Ctrl+H
Expand search to desktop	Ctrl+Alt+K

Table 1-4. General Keyboard Shortcuts for Creating Outlook Items

Item to Be Created	Shortcut
Appointment	Ctrl+Shift+A
Contact	Ctrl+Shift+C
Distribution list	Ctrl+Shift+L
Fax	Ctrl+Shift+X
Folder	Ctrl+Shift+E
Journal entry	Ctrl+Shift+J
Meeting request	Ctrl+Shift+Q
Email message	Ctrl+Shift+M
Note	Ctrl+Shift+N
Document	Ctrl+Shift+H
Search folder	Ctrl+Shift+P
Task	Ctrl+Shift+K
Task request	Ctrl+Shift+U
Post to folder	Ctrl+Shift+S
Post a reply	Ctrl+T

Table 1-5. General Keyboard Shortcuts for Manipulating Items

Action	Shortcut
Save	Ctrl+S
Save and close	Alt+S
Save as	F12
Undo	Ctrl+Z
Delete	Ctrl+D
Print	Ctrl+P
Copy item	Ctrl+Shift+Y
Move item	Ctrl+Shift+V
Check name	Ctrl+K
Spell check	F7
Flag for follow-up	Ctrl+Shift+G
Forward	Ctrl+F
Send to all	Alt+S
Turn on editing in a field	F2
Left align	Ctrl+L
Center align	Ctrl+E
Right align	Ctrl+R

Table 1-6. Most Commonly Used Shortcuts in Email

Action	Shortcut
Switch to inbox	Ctrl+Shift+I
Switch to outbox	Ctrl+Shift+O
Send	Alt+S
Reply	Ctrl+R
Reply all	Ctrl+Shift+R
Forward	Ctrl+F
Forward as attachment	Ctrl+Alt+F
Mark as not junk mail	Ctrl+Alt+J
Check for new messages	F9
Create new message (when in Mail)	Ctrl+N

Action	Shortcut
Create new message from anywhere in Outlook	Ctrl+Shift+M
Open a message	Ctrl+O
Open address book	Ctrl+Shift+B
Toggle follow-up flag	Insert
Mark as read	Ctrl+Q
Mark as unread	Ctrl+U
Find or replace	F4
Find next	Shift+F4
Print	Ctrl+P
Mark for download	Ctrl+Alt+M
Clear Mark for Download	Ctrl+Alt+U
Display send/receive progress	Ctrl+B

Table 1-7. Most Commonly Used Shortcuts in Calendar

Action	Shortcut
Create a new appointment	Ctrl+N
Create a new appointment from anywhere in Outlook	Ctrl+Shift+A
Create a new meeting request	Ctrl+Shift+Q
Forward item	Ctrl+F
Reply to meeting request with a message	Ctrl+R
Reply all	Ctrl+Shift+R
Show from 1 to 10 days in the calendar	Alt+1, Alt+2, and so on, through to Alt+0 (for 10)
Go to date	Ctrl+G
Switch to weeks	Alt+– (minus sign)
Switch to months	Alt+= (equals sign)
Month view	Ctrl+Alt+4
Next/previous day	Ctrl+right arrow/left arrow
Next/previous week	Alt+down arrow/up arrow
Next/previous month	Alt+Page Down/Page Up
Start of week	Alt+Home

Continued

Table 1-7. *Continued*

Action	Shortcut
End of week	Alt+End
Full week view	Ctrl+Alt+3
Work week view	Ctrl+Alt+2
Next/previous appointment	Ctrl+. (period)/Ctrl+, (comma)
Set up recurring appointment	Ctrl+G
Select time that working day begins/ends	Home/End
Select previous/next block of time	Up arrow/down arrow
Select block of time at top of screen	Page Up
Select block of time at bottom of screen	Page Down
Extend/reduce time	Shift+up arrow/Shift+down arrow
Move appointment up/down	Alt+up arrow/Alt+down arrow
Move appointment forward one week	Alt+down arrow
Move appointment back one week	Alt+up arrow

Table 1-8. Most Commonly Used Shortcuts in Contacts

Action	Shortcut
Dial a contact	Ctrl+Shift+D
Find a contact	F3
Search address book	F11
Select all contacts	Ctrl+A
New email for selected contact	Ctrl+F
New Journal entry for selected contact	Ctrl+J
New contact	Ctrl+N
New contact from anywhere in Outlook	Ctrl+Shift+C
Open contact	Ctrl+O
Close contact	Esc
Open address book	Ctrl+Shift+B

Table 1-9. Most Commonly Used Shortcuts in Tasks

Action	Shortcut
Display or hide the To-Do Bar	Alt+F2
Accept task request	Alt+C
Decline task request	Alt+D
Find task	Ctrl+E
Open the Go to Folder window	Ctrl+Y
New task	Ctrl+N
New task from anywhere in Outlook	Ctrl+Shift+K
New task request	Ctrl+Shift+U
Forward a task as attachment	Ctrl+F
Open selected task as journal item	Ctrl+J
Mark task as complete	Insert

CHAPTER 2

Messaging

This chapter is all about getting the most out of Outlook messaging, which builds on the well-cited paradigm of enhanced workflow and organization. We'll take you through how to enhance the send/receive experience with templates and rules, how Outlook integrates with Windows Live Messenger, and how to send and receive faxes; we'll finish up with a section about how to access Outlook remotely using Outlook Anywhere.

Using Helpful Sending and Receiving Tools

Aside from the most obvious features of sending and receiving email, a few extras in Outlook will improve your overall workflow capability. The following procedures allow you to work better and faster:

- You can automatically send a copy of all email messages you send to a specified recipient.
- You can use a template to force the use of a specific message format.
- You can expire an email to downgrade its relevance after a certain date.
- You can prevent recipients from using the Reply to All or Forward command with a custom email form.
- You can use the Out Of Office Assistant to send an automatic response to anyone emailing you.

Automatically Sending All Email to a Specified Recipient

Sometimes you might require that all emails sent from your system be automatically copied to another recipient. For example, if you work in a sales office, you might want all the emails you send to customers to be automatically sent to your manager as well. In this way, if you were out of the office on vacation, your manager could deal with some of your customers' inquiries.

As you can no doubt imagine, Outlook has a variety of ways to accomplish this; however, the simplest and quickest way to set this up is to use a rule that CCs a specified recipient on all email. The procedure to set this up is as follows:

1. Select the Tools menu, and then choose Rules and Alerts.

2. Click the New Rule button, start from a blank rule, and select Check Messages After Sending. Click Next.

3. Don't choose any sending conditions, click Next to apply this rule to all outgoing messages, and then confirm your action by clicking Yes (see Figure 2-1).

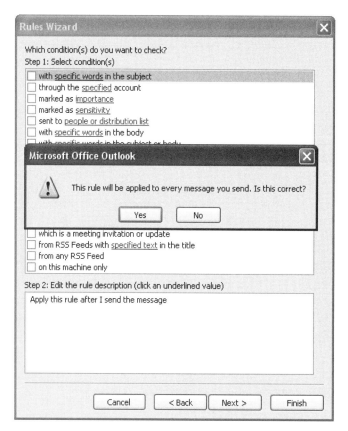

Figure 2-1. Confirm you want this rule applied to all outbound messages.

4. On the next screen, select Cc the Message to People or Distribution List, and then click the hyperlink for People or Distribution List in the lower part of the dialog box. When you see the Rule Address dialog box, select the intended recipients. Click OK. Back in the Rules Wizard, click Next.

5. If you want to include any exceptions, add them at this stage. For example, to use an exception to make this rule more useful, you could have a distribution list with all your friends' and family's emails and create an exception for that list in this rule. In that way, you could be sure that only work-related email will be copied to your manager. When you're ready, click Next.

6. Finally, on the last page of the Rules Wizard, give the rule a meaningful name, and select Turn On This Rule. Click Finish.

Using Templates to Facilitate More Versatile Email Distribution

Distribution lists are fantastic for grouping the email addresses of recipients to whom you regularly send emails. However, the biggest problem with distribution lists is that they are assigned as a single entity in the standard New ➤ Mail Message form; hence, the distribution list recipients will be addressed as To, CC, or BCC.

If you want to construct a more complicated distribution list, with some recipients on the To field, some recipients on the CC field, and yet more recipients on the BCC field, you have to use a message template where you explicitly assign recipients to each field.

The following procedure guides you through the process of creating an email template:

1. Start to create a new message as you would normally.

2. Fill in the To, CC, and BCC address fields with the recipients you require. You can customize the email in any way you like, with a standard subject line, some standard heading in the message body, or an elaborate checklist that you will fill in each time you send it (see Figure 2-2).

3. When you've finished constructing your template, click the Microsoft Office Button, and then select Save As. Where you see Save As Type at the bottom of the Save As dialog box, use the drop-down list to select Outlook Template (*.oft). Give the template a meaningful name, and then click Save.

4. You can close the email since the template is now stored for later use (unless you need to use it right away).

5. To create a message using this template, click the Tools menu, select Forms, and then click Choose Form.

6. When you see the Choose Form dialog box, open the Look In drop-down list, and then select User Templates in File System.

7. Highlight the template you saved earlier (see Figure 2-3), and then click Open.

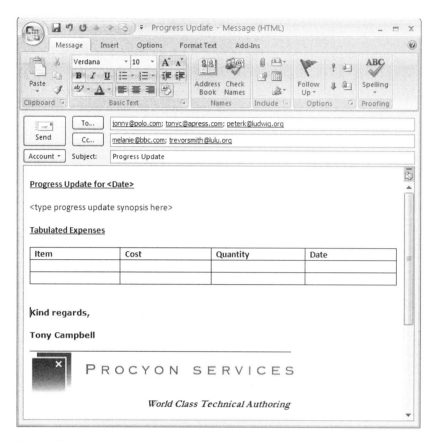

Figure 2-2. An email template can be as elaborate as you require.

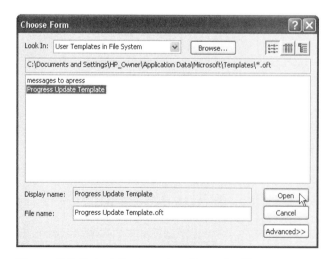

Figure 2-3. Select the template from the file system.

A new email window will now appear based on the information you typed earlier. You can add any new information you require, leaving the standard formatting and recipient addresses intact.

Assigning Expiration Dates

Sometimes it's important to be able to assign an expiration date on a time-critical email and therefore downgrade the message's importance after that date. When a message expires in Outlook, the message header remains visible in your Outlook folder but appears with a strikethrough, designating it as expired. Nevertheless, you can still open and read the message.

To expire an email after a certain date and time, follow these steps:

1. Start creating your email in the usual way.

2. On the Options tab, in the More Options group, click the small arrow in the bottom-right corner to open the Message Options dialog box, shown in Figure 2-4.

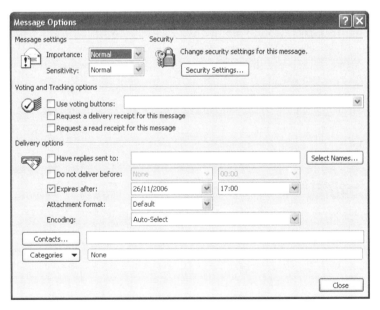

Figure 2-4. Use the Message Options dialog box to expire an email after a particular date and time.

3. Select the Expires After checkbox, and then select the appropriate date and time for the message to expire. Click Close.

Using the Out Of Office Assistant

If you are an Exchange Server user, a useful rule you can switch on when you are planning to be away from the office is the Out Of Office Assistant. This feature is available in the Tools menu when you are using an Exchange Server account. Clicking it permits you to type a short message that is automatically sent to anyone who sends you an email when the rule is enabled. Use this message as a means to tell your colleagues and customers when you will return to the office and who to contact in the case of an inquiry being unable to wait for your return.

> **NOTE** The Out Of Office Assistant option appears only when you are using an Exchange Server account.

Preventing Recipients from Using Reply to All

You've probably seen it a dozen times—a corporate announcement goes out and some witty employee decides to use Reply to All with some meaningless banter as a way of showing how clever they can be. This bombarding of the email system can soon fill up inboxes with garbage and is certainly worth preventing if you can.

To ensure recipients cannot simply hit the Reply to All button when you've sent an email to a large distribution list, you can create a custom form that removes this capability. You can then use this form to create your corporate announcement. To do so, follow this procedure:

1. Select the Tools menu, and then choose Forms ➤ Design a Form.
2. In the Standard Forms Library (see Figure 2-5), select Message, and then click Open.

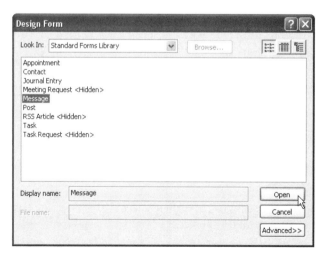

Figure 2-5. Customize the standard message form to remove the Reply to All functionality.

3. Click the Actions tab on the far right of the tabbed list (above the address bar), and then highlight the Reply to All row, as shown in Figure 2-6.

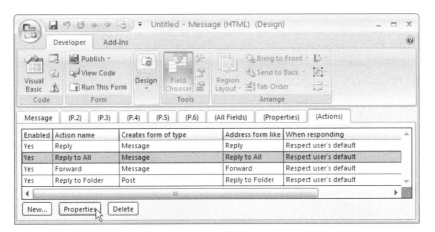

Figure 2-6. Select the appropriate command you want to modify (in this case Reply to All).

4. Click the Properties button, uncheck the Enabled setting, and then click OK.

5. Now click the Properties tab (see Figure 2-7), and select Send Form Definition with Item. When you see the warning advising that this is not good practice, ignore it; in this case, it is OK, so click OK.

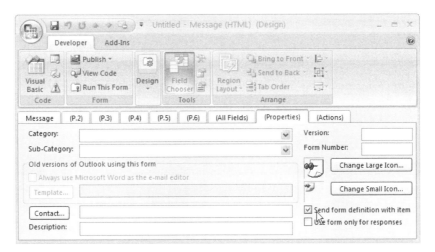

Figure 2-7. Sending the definition ensures the Reply to All feature is disabled on the recipient's system.

6. Next, click the Publish button on the Ribbon at the top of the message window, and then select Publish Form As.

7. In the Publish Form As dialog box, ensure the Look In drop-down list is showing Personal Forms Library; then in the Display Name textbox, type a meaningful name for your new custom form, such as **Reply All Disabled**. In the Form Name textbox, type a system name for the form with no spaces included in the title, such as **NoReplyAll**. Click Publish.

8. Back on the design form, click the Microsoft Office Button, and select Close.

That's it. You've now created a new message form you can use the next time you want to send out an email with the Reply to All functionality disabled.

To use the form, select Tools ➤ Forms ➤ Choose a Form. When you see the Choose Form dialog box, shown in Figure 2-8, open the Look In drop-down list, and then select Personal Forms Library.

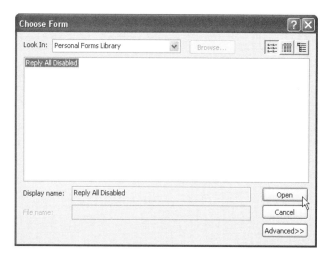

Figure 2-8. Select your custom form from the personal forms library.

Highlight your custom form (in this case Reply All Disabled), and then click Open. You can now create your message as usual and send it. When it's received, as long as the recipients are using Outlook, the Reply to All function will be disabled.

Being Your Own SMTP Server (Windows XP Only)

Sending email via Exchange Server is easy since your Exchange Server administrator will undoubtedly configure Outlook to connect to the appropriate server, which automatically takes care of business when you hit the Send button. If you're using an ISP account and your ISP provides an SMTP service, they will supply you with the SMTP server's address and account logon details, allowing Outlook, yet again, to take care of business. But what happens when you are connectivity challenged (away from your Exchange Server) or are accessing the Internet via a service that does not allow a direct connection to your ISP, such as in a WiFi hotspot in an airport?

Never fear, there is a solution. You can use an extremely underused service that's included in Windows XP Professional: the SMTP service.

Using this service, you can send email via your very own PC, without having to route email through anyone else's server. In this way, the email will be sent directly to the recipient's email server without having to first pass through an intermediary.

Sounds fantastic, doesn't it? But there is a downside: many email servers won't accept email from an unknown SMTP server (and this, in effect, is what your computer has become), believing them to be responsible for the proliferation of spam. Anyhow, in the majority of cases, you can use such a system, but it will certainly be the case that some email will not get through other people's antispam settings.

The SMTP service comes as part of Internet Information Services (IIS), which is a workstation Internet server capable of hosting your own website. Nevertheless, this section deals only with email and SMTP since web services and IIS are topics that could fill books themselves.

As a prerequisite for using this service, you might want to create a separate account or Outlook profile you can use for this purpose. In this way, you can easily switch between your regular mode of operation (connecting to your Exchange Server or ISP) and this away-from-home mode that sends via your own system.

> **CAUTION** Always check with your network administrator before installing IIS in case corporate policy prohibits you from running your own SMTP capability on your workstation. In many cases, running an SMTP service outside the control of corporate governance is deemed unacceptable from a security standpoint since SMTP servers generally make attack vectors for hackers looking for routes into your system.

The procedure for setting up the SMTP service on a Windows XP computer is as follows:

1. Click the Start menu, and then select Control Panel.
2. Select Add or Remove Programs, and then click Add/Remove Windows Components.
3. Select Internet Information Services from the list, and then click Details.
4. Select SMTP, and then click OK.
5. Click Next, and then follow the procedure for installing the SMTP service.
6. Once the installation is complete, return to the Control Panel, and select Administrative Tools ➤ Internet Information Services.
7. In the management console for IIS, right-click Default Web Site, and then choose Properties.
8. Focus on the Directory Security tab, and then click Edit in Anonymous Access and Authentication Control. Uncheck the Anonymous Access option, and then click OK. Click OK again to close the Properties dialog box.
9. Now click Relay, select Only The List Below, and then select Allow All Computers Which Successfully Authenticate to Relay, Regardless of the List Above. Click OK, and then click OK again to close the SMTP Properties dialog box.
10. Now you can open Outlook and navigate to the account you have configured for use with your local SMTP server. In the Outgoing Mail Server (SMTP) box, type **localhost**. Type the incoming server name as you usually would, and then type the login information for that incoming server, as shown in Figure 2-9.

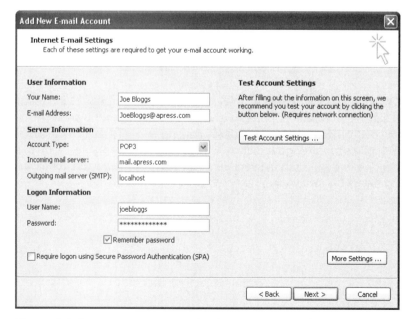

Figure 2-9. Instruct outgoing mail to be sent via your local computer

11. Finally, click More Settings, and then select the Outgoing Server tab in the Internet E-mail Settings dialog box. Select My Outgoing Server (SMTP) Requires Authentication, then select Log On Using, and finally type the username and password you usually use to log in to your system. Click OK, and then click Test Account Settings. The send and receive should come back successfully if you've accurately followed these steps.

12. Finally, click Next, and then click Finish to close the Change E-mail Account Wizard.

If you find you are receiving message delivery failures from certain recipients using this method of sending, the recipient's email server is undoubtedly performing a security check on your system and blocking your send attempts. These is no easy way around this; instead, you may have to try sending email to that particular set of recipients using another method, such as Windows Live Mail (previously Hotmail) or Google Mail.

Integrating with Windows Live Messenger

If you're a keen user of online chat (often referred to as *instant messaging*), you'll be pleased to know Outlook integrates seamlessly with the latest Microsoft instant messaging client, known as Windows Live Messenger. This is part of the overall Windows Live initiative (`http://get.live.com/`) that includes a variety of useful Internet capabilities, such as Hotmail's successor, called Windows Live Mail, and Windows Live Spaces, which is a personal blog site. Figure 2-10 shows Windows Live Messenger.

> **NOTE** Windows Live Messenger provides a whole lot more than simple text-based messaging. You can also strike up a video call using a webcam, play interactive games with your contacts over the Internet, securely exchange files, and make phone calls using an IP telephony service known as Windows Live Call (Microsoft's answer to the hugely successful Skype system).

Once you've installed Windows Live Messenger, you'll have to populate the contacts database with people you want to chat with. This is really easy using the Windows Live Contacts window (you'll find this by clicking the green icon to the right of the Find a Contact or Number box), as shown in Figure 2-11.

Figure 2-10. Instantly send messages to contacts using Windows Live Messenger

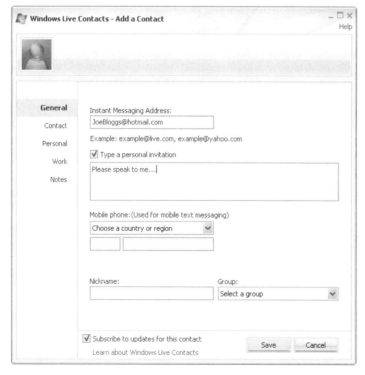

Figure 2-11. Adding contacts to the Windows Live Messenger makes them available in Outlook.

Once you've paired your Outlook contacts to your Windows Live Messenger contacts, you'll start to see some new facilities available in Outlook that you might not have noticed before.

If a contact is signed into Windows Live Messenger, you'll see a green icon next to their name on any emails you've received from them, and the green icon will also appear in that person's Outlook contact item next to the email address, as shown in Figure 2-12.

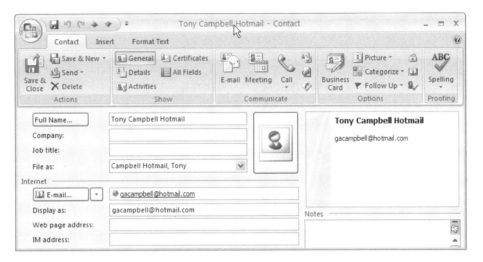

Figure 2-12. The green icon shows that a contact is signed into Windows Live Messenger.

If you right-click the email address of a user who has a green icon showing on an email from that user, you'll see a notification at the top of the context menu stating that the user is online and available, and you can click the following options: Reply with Instant Message or Reply All with Instant Message. Choosing Reply with Instant Message will open a Windows Live Messenger chat window and allow you to start communicating.

Using Windows Fax and Scan

The Windows Fax and Scan service included with Windows Vista provides the capability for both faxing and scanning documents. You can use this feature to send and receive faxes directly from Outlook, replacing the somewhat inadequate predecessor (Fax Services) provided by Windows XP.

> **NOTE** The Windows Fax and Scan service is provided in three of the Vista
> SKUs by default: Ultimate, Enterprise, and Business.

In the following sections, we'll cover how to use the Windows Fax and Scan service to send and receive faxes directly from your local computer. Enterprise fax systems exist and are commonly provided as a server-based solution, but you can just as easily do all this using your own computer and a fax-capable modem.

Figure 2-13 shows the basic Windows Fax and Scan interface.

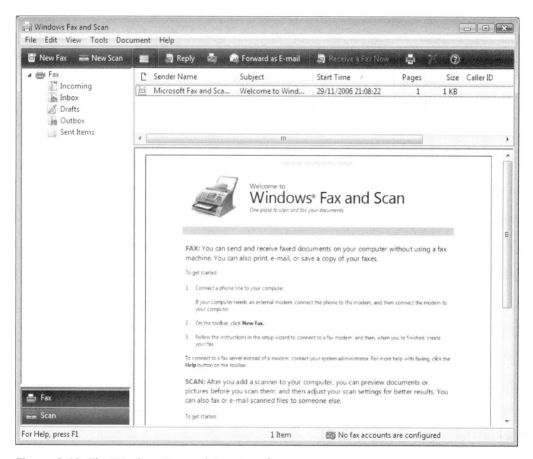

Figure 2-13. The Windows Fax and Scan interface

Sending Faxes

The first time you send a new fax, you'll be prompted to set up the fax program:

1. In Windows Fax and Scan, click the New Fax button at the top-left corner.

2. The Choose a Fax Modem or Server screen appears; for the purposes of this section, choose Connect to a Fax Modem.

3. On the next screen, type a name that will help you identify the modem you're using to send faxes.

4. The Choose How to Receive Faxes screen appears; on this screen you can choose to have Windows Fax and Scan answer all incoming calls as faxes automatically, notify you when incoming calls are received in order to begin receiving faxes, or defer the decision and move on with sending a fax right now. Choose the Notify Me option for the purposes of this section.

Receiving Faxes

Receiving faxes operates in much the same way. Faxes you receive from a fax modem are stored in the Windows Fax and Scan inbox. You can then take them from the inbox and save them in another location that you prefer.

When you first send a fax, you were taken through a wizard that configures the incoming fax settings. You can change those settings by selecting Tools ➤ Fax Settings.

Figure 2-14 shows the Fax Settings dialog box and the appropriate options to configure.

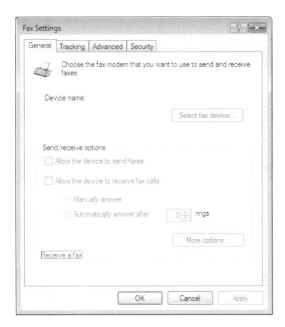

Figure 2-14. Changing fax receipt options

If you have configured Windows to notify you about incoming calls so you can choose to receive them as a fax, Windows will pop up a notification window in the corner of your screen alerting you to an incoming call. You can receive the fax by clicking the notification bubble, or while the incoming call is ringing, you can choose the Receive a Fax Now option from the toolbar at the top of the window.

> **TIP** You can tell Windows Fax and Scan to automatically save a copy of each received fax. Choose Tools ➤ Fax Settings, and then click the More Options button on the General tab. Check the Save a Copy *to* checkbox, and then enter the path to the folder where you want to store received faxes.

Faxing in Outlook

From Outlook, you can send faxes in a few different ways. You can print any item directly to the fax modem (using the Windows Fax and Scan service) by clicking the File button and selecting Print. Then, in the Print dialog box, select Fax from the Name drop-down list, as shown in Figure 2-15. Now, all you need to do is follow the procedures outlined previously to complete the fax transmission.

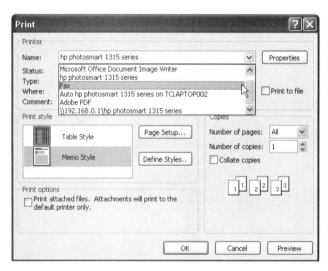

Figure 2-15. Select the Fax printer to route an item to the Windows Fax and Scan service.

Alternatively, if you open the New menu, you'll notice an item at the bottom entitled Internet Fax. If you click this, you'll be notified that you need to sign up with a fax service provider. If you click OK, Internet Explorer fires up and takes you to Office Online where you'll see a list of available online faxing services to which you can subscribe. Using these services, you will be sending faxes via an Internet fax-relay service rather than your local modem, and you will be able to receive faxes as email attachments, using a real telephone number, that the fax service provider receives and then forwards to your email.

Using Outlook Anywhere

If you are connecting Outlook to an Exchange Server (requires Exchange Server 2003 or later), you can exploit a feature of Outlook that allows you to connect to the server using the Internet protocol HTTP. Usually, when you connect Outlook to your Exchange Server across a local area network, you use a network protocol called a Remote Procedure Call (RPC). However, if you are operating your system outside the corporate firewall (such as dialing in from a hotel room to an ISP), you have only two alternatives: using a virtual private network (VPN) or using Outlook Anywhere.

Some corporations provide VPN access to remote workers, but Microsoft has provided Outlook Anywhere to make up for those who do not have a VPN service. Effectively, Outlook Anywhere allows you to connect to your Exchange Server using the RPC protocol (as if you were inside the firewall), but this is carried through the corporate firewall over HTTP. This means that, using a standard firewall configuration for web browsing, you can get remote access to Exchange Server from Outlook with nothing but plain old Internet access.

Chapter 12 covers configuring Outlook Anywhere.

> **CAUTION** This service is available only on systems that are running Windows XP with Service Pack 2 or later; in other words, if you're running Vista, you're fine!

Message Organization

To fully appreciate the value of Outlook as an organizational aid, you need to employ a variety of key facilities to help you sift, group, and consume information. This chapter will train you in using these features, scrutinizing the following functionality:

- Outlook search folders allow you to view items matching specific search criteria.
- Creating multiple accounts lets you separate information into categories or segregate information from different sources.
- Using Outlook rules and alerts lets you automatically process items into categories, assign them to folders, and be notified when specific events have occurred.
- Outlook's junk email filter lets you remove clutter from your inbox.
- Using send/receive groups means you can process messages selectively.

Using Search Folders

Outlook provides a useful way of grouping information with similar characteristics and allowing this information to be sorted into containers known as *search folders*. Search folders are simply views into the mail store based on predefined rules (search criteria) that you create from a variety of item attributes.

> **NOTE** Don't confuse search folders with Outlook's new instant search facility that allows you to quickly locate any item in the information store without having to trawl through reams of emails, folders, contacts, notes, and contacts. The instant search requires that Windows components are installed on your system before it can function. For Windows XP users, you'll need to install the Windows Desktop Search component (available from http://www.microsoft.com/downloads). If you don't have it installed, a dialog box prompts you to download and install it. Windows Vista includes the Windows Desktop Search component by default, and it's automatically enabled for you. If you decide you don't want to use instant search, you can still search your information store, but performance and functionality will be limited.

Search folders appear on the Navigation pane on the left side of the screen with three created with the default installation as follows:

- Categorized Mail
- Large Mail
- Unread Mail

Categorized Mail will display all email items that have a category assigned. *Large Mail* will display all email items that are larger than 100KB (although you can change this threshold if you want). *Unread Mail* will show you all the emails in your mail store that haven't yet been processed (or ones you've since marked as unread to return to later). Figure 3-1 shows these default search folders.

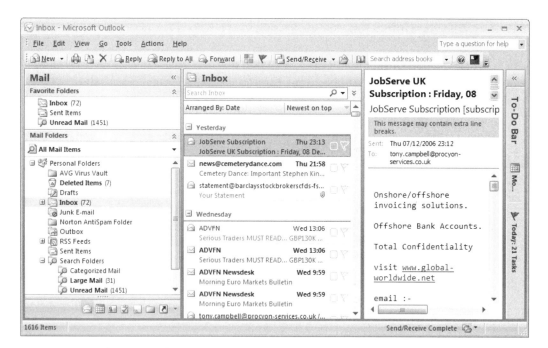

Figure 3-1. Outlook provides three search folders by default.

> **TIP** The Large Mail search folder is particularly useful if you happen to exceed your mailbox quota (specifically for Exchange users). You can use this to quickly assess which items are causing the problem so you can rectify it as soon as possible.

Search folders are created within the parent data file, such as a personal folder file (a .pst file) and will not pull data from multiple data files. This means each search folder you create will apply to only one data file.

In addition to the default search folders displayed in the Navigation pane, Outlook provides a set of predefined search folders you can expose and add to the displayed list.

If you right-click the top level of the Search Folders node in the Navigation pane and select New Search Folder, you'll see the dialog box shown in Figure 3-2.

Figure 3-2. Add predefined search folders to the list in the Navigation pane using the New Search Folder dialog box.

> **NOTE** Search folders are simply views of the email message store rather than physical containers. Therefore, deleting a search folder will not delete the messages contained within it.

To add one of these search folders to the Navigation pane, highlight the one you are interested in, and then check the criteria in the Customize Search Folder box that meets your requirements, such as the 100KB limit on the Large Mail search folder. Also, make sure the search folder is being applied to the correct data file. You can check this because it's listed next to the Search Mail In list. When you're done, click OK.

You can modify the criteria for any of the predefined search folders by highlighting the folder you are interested in and then clicking the Choose button in the Customize Search Folder box. In the example shown in Figure 3-3, you'll see we've upped the mail size threshold from the default 100KB to 200KB for the Large Mail search folder.

Figure 3-3. Customize the predefined search folder criteria to suit your own requirements.

To create a new search folder from scratch, scroll to the bottom of the New Search Folder dialog box, highlight Create a Custom Search Folder, and then click Choose. When you see the Custom Search Folder dialog box, shown in Figure 3-4, type a meaningful name for the search folder, and then click Criteria.

Figure 3-4. Create a custom search folder from scratch for absolute control over its purpose.

The Search Folder Criteria dialog box offers a vast array of characteristics you can use to create the query that forms the basis of the content in your search folder. You have the option of searching for specific words and specifying where in the message to look, such as in the subject field, in the message body, or in frequently used text fields (see Figure 3-5).

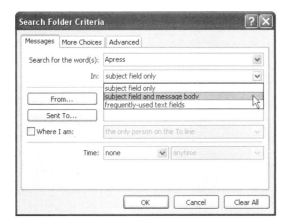

Figure 3-5. Create a search folder based on a search for a specific word or phrase.

You can instruct the search folder to interrogate the messages from or sent to a discrete set of users using the From and Sent To buttons, and if you select the Where I Am checkbox, you can choose from the following three possibilities:

- The Only Person on the To Line
- On the To Line with Other People
- On the CC Line with Other people

You can also make the content of the search folder time-critical by selecting Received, Sent, Due, Expires, Created, or Modified in the Time list and applying one of the time-related qualifiers from the following: Anytime, Yesterday, Today, Tomorrow, In the Last 7 Days, In the Next 7 Days, Last Week, This Week, Next Week, Last Month, This Month, and Next Month.

The More Choices tab (see Figure 3-6) allows you to filter based on Outlook color categories, matched further against a range of other criteria.

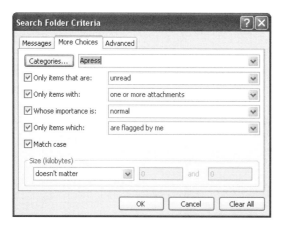

Figure 3-6. Filter your search folder contents on Outlook color categories.

The Advanced tab allows you to construct your own specialized queries based on any number of the hundreds of attributes associated with all types of Outlook items. These attributes are made available by clicking the Field button and then selecting from the drop-down lists. It's worthwhile to trawl through the available fields to see just how convoluted you can make your search folders.

Using Rules to Sort Your Messages

One of the finest features of Outlook is the ability to perform actions automatically on emails that arrive in your inbox. To do this, you must define *rules* that govern what happens when an email is received; a rule can be as simple as moving an email to a specific folder, or it can be as elaborate as first replying to the message with a standard response, flagging it for follow-up, categorizing it, forwarding a copy to another mail account, and then filing it for use later in a backup folder. Practically anything is possible using rules, and this section's goal is to delve deep into the depths of rule creation to get you beyond simple into the most elaborate of protocols.

To start, take a look at the standard Rules and Alerts dialog box by selecting Tools ➤ Rules and Alerts (see Figure 3-7).

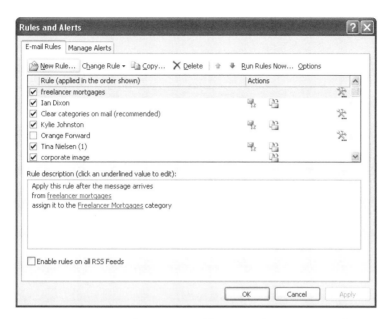

Figure 3-7. Create rules to control how email is automatically handled by Outlook.

> **NOTE** Every action taken by a rule has an associated symbol. These symbols appear next to each rule in the Rules and Alerts dialog box to give you a quick overview of the functionality associated with each rule. To see exactly what each rule does, the rule description at the bottom of the window explains it in plain English.

Outlook always applies rules in the order shown in the Rule list, so if you have more than one rule that needs to be applied to any individual email fitting your criteria, you will need to ensure later rules always remain cognizant of former rules in case emails are modified. To change the way rules are processed, highlight whichever rule you are interested in, and then use the up and down arrows to change its position. When you click OK, Outlook will put the new order into practice.

To create a new rule, click the New Rule button. This starts the Rules Wizard, shown in Figure 3-8; you can follow it screen by screen to add whichever criteria suit your needs.

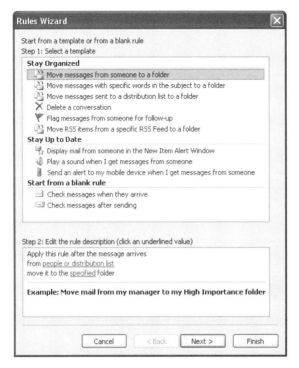

Figure 3-8. Use the Rules Wizard to simplify the process of creating a rule.

> **TIP** The Rules Wizard has a predefined list of the most commonly created rules already defined. All you have to do is select one from the list, such as Move Messages from Someone to a Folder, and fill in the names of the some-one and the folder.

To best illustrate rule creation, we'll walk you through the process of creating a complicated set of actions we use when we receive new messages from a contact called Joe Bloggs. When Joe sends an email, we want him to receive a response that we're available and working on his request, and then we want the message forwarded to our boss before notifying us that a new message from Joe has arrived in the inbox. Finally, we want that message moved to a special folder for all of Joe's email, called Messages from Joe. So, let's get started:

1. We won't be using the predefined rules for this particular example since we've opted to create quite a complicated chain of events that need to occur when this message arrives. Under the Start from a Blank Rule heading on the first page of the Rules Wizard, select Check Messages When They Arrive, and then click Next.

2. On the screen shown in Figure 3-9, select the From People or Distribution List condition. The rule condition will be added to the Step 2 box at the bottom of the screen. Click People or Distribution List. When you see the Rule Address dialog box, locate the contact name from your Address Book that pertains to this rule (in this case Joe Bloggs), and then click OK. Back in the Rules Wizard, click Next.

Figure 3-9. Start by selecting the condition against which you want to check.

3. You are now asked to specify what actions you'd like Outlook to take when you receive a message matching the previous criterion. Referring to our requirements, we want the following to happen: move it to the specified folder, assign it to the category, forward it to people or distribution list, reply using a specific template, and play a sound. In each case, you need to click the blue, underlined hyperlink in the lower part of the Rules Wizard dialog box to specify each action; for example, clicking the Category hyperlink will allow you to choose from the list of already defined color categories. When you're ready, click Next.

4. You now have the option to add exceptions to this rule in case you want to further filter on specific words, recipients, sensitivity, importance, and so on. Figure 3-10 shows the exception list. When you've added any exceptions (none in the case of this example), click Next.

> **NOTE** If you want Outlook to also apply your email rules to RSS items, you can select Enable Rules on All RSS Feeds at the bottom of the Rules and Alerts dialog box.

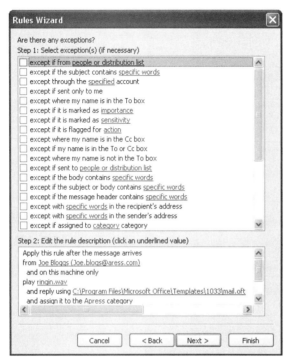

Figure 3-10. Add rule exceptions if there are circumstances when you don't want the rule run.

5. On the Finish Rule Setup page, give the rule a meaningful name; then, before you click Finish, decide whether you'd like the rule run on your current inbox or whether you want this run only on new email arriving. Be warned, however, that if you have a lot of emails in your inbox that apply to this rule, then you might end up processing your inbox for a very long time. When you're done, click Finish.

Using the Junk Mail Filter

Junk mail has to be the bane of the Internet, with more and more rubbish permeating our inboxes every day. Luckily, the biggest brains in the industry are trying to crack this problem both at the server and client ends, and it's the junk email filter in Outlook that helps protect Office users from this annoyance.

To access and configure the junk email filter, select Tools ➤ Junk E-mail on the Preferences tab. This opens the Junk E-mail Options dialog box, as shown in Figure 3-11.

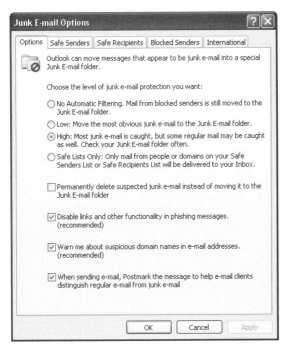

Figure 3-11. Configure how Outlook handles junk email.

The junk email filter will give you four levels of protection:

No Automatic Filtering: All email received is considered safe and will appear in your inbox. This setting will still allow Outlook to move messages from blocked senders to the Junk E-mail folder.

Low: If you set the junk email filter to Low protection, only email with an obvious junk mail signature will be moved to the Junk E-mail folder. This is a predefined specification and is not very clever. You can augment the Low setting by creating your own Blocked Senders list rules.

High: This setting will capture most junk email; however, it may also catch messages that are not junk, and you'll have to make sure you occasionally check your Junk E-mail folder to ensure you have not missed a legitimate message. If you see a message that should not have been in the Junk E-mail folder, right-click the message, select Junk E-mail from the context menu, and then select Add Sender to Safe Senders List (see Figure 3-12).

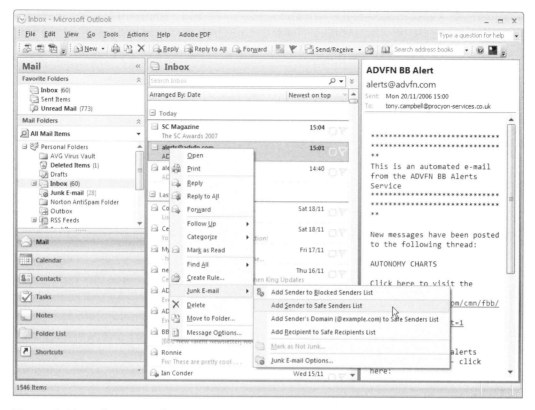

Figure 3-12. Make sure no legitimate messages go to the Junk E-mail folder.

Safe Lists Only: This is the strictest of all the settings and ensures that only emails received from senders who you already have added to your Safe Senders list or Safe Recipients list will be allowed into your inbox.

The default setting in Outlook 2007 is High; however, with the current volume of spam bombarding us day in and day out, Safe Lists Only is becoming more and more attractive.

> **CAUTION** You have the option of permanently deleting junk email rather than sending it to the Junk E-mail folder, but we don't recommend this since the filter is not by any means perfect and because you may end up deleting email from a legitimate source.

A new feature in Outlook 2007 is that of the *postmark*, which helps fight the blight by adding a small digital stamp to your emails that is processed when the email is sent from your outbox and received in another user's inbox. This digital postmark allows Outlook to better judge the origin of the email and whether it was really intended for you or has come in by chance. The war on spam has just begun, and this postmarking will certainly not stop it; however, it's yet another weapon in the arsenal and will deter the worst offenders. This feature is turned on by default. To switch the postmark off, if you are legitimately sending bulk loads of email, select Tools ➤ Options, and then on the Preferences tab, under E-mail, click Junk E-mail. Clear the following checkbox: *When sending e-mail, postmark the message to help recipient e-mail programs distinguish regular e-mail from junk e-mail.*

> **NOTE** The postmark feature relies on the fact that the overhead the post-mark imposes on the system will seriously affect the ability to bulk send email. It should not affect standard email users; it will affect only those automating the sending of vast numbers of emails programmatically.

Back in the Junk E-mail Options dialog box, if you click the Safe Senders tab, you'll see a list of email addresses you consider friendly. To add new addresses to the list, click the Add button, and type the address; alternatively, right-click an email in your inbox (or Junk E-mail folder), and select Add Sender to Safe Senders List. You can export your Safe Senders list to a text file and share it with another user (you can email it to her). If you receive a Safe Senders list from another user, you can import it using the Import from File command. If you want Outlook to automatically populate this list with recipients you send emails to, select Automatically Add People I E-mail to the Safe Senders List. The Safe Recipients list is similar to the Safe Senders list in that email addresses or domain names specified on this list are never considered junk mail.

Blocked Senders is a list of email addresses and domain names that are always treated as junk email. To add a new blocked sender to the list, click the Add button, and then type the email address or domain name you want to block.

Many junk emails can be determined as such by their country of origin. If you click the International tab on the Junk E-mail Options dialog box, you'll see two buttons: Blocked Top-Level Domain List and Blocked Encodings List. If you are positive you want to block all mail originating in a certain country or containing a specific type of character encoding such as Western European, Korean, or Baltic, you can edit these lists accordingly (see Figure 3-13 and Figure 3-14).

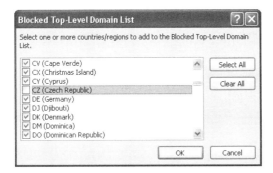

Figure 3-13. The blocked country list

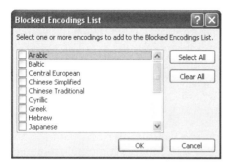

Figure 3-14. The blocked encoding (language) list

Using Send/Receive Groups

Outlook allows you to process messages on your mail server before they are ever downloaded to your system, saving long download times over slow connections and allowing you to be highly selective in which information you really require.

You can configure Outlook in a variety of ways to facilitate this selective processing of email through what are known as *send/receive groups* that allow you to specify how email is handled between Outlook and your server, be it on an ISP or on a corporate Exchange server.

The following sections cover setting up and configuring send/receive groups to help you be more selective in which messages you choose to download and how you treat messages that remain on the server.

Understanding Remote Mail

Three types of remote mail exist:

- Remote mail on an Exchange server
- Remote mail on an ISP (using POP3)
- Remote mail on a web server, such as Hotmail, using HTTP or IMAP

In both the Exchange and HTTP/IMAP scenarios, you can specify which email should be downloaded and which email should remain on (or be deleted from) the server. In terms of Exchange, email is usually stored on the server, so the concept of remote mail really comes into its own only when you are running in cached mode. If you are using an HTTP/IMAP email service, you have the option of working offline and synchronizing with the server when you establish a connection. With regard to a POP3 ISP service, it's possible to instruct Outlook to download only those messages you believe to be required after viewing only the header. You can opt to keep a copy of the message on the server if you desire, and you can place an expiration time on messages kept on the server to force them to be deleted after a certain duration.

> **NOTE** Remote mail is focused on you first downloading all message headers to Outlook, determining which ones are the ones you really need at that time, and then instructing Outlook to selectively download only those you have selected.

To download only the message headers for a specific mail account, select Tools ➤ Send/Receive, and then select the mail account you want to download headers from; in the example in Figure 3-15, we've chosen "Download Procyon Service" Only. Then select Download Inbox Headers.

> **NOTE** You'll have to make sure you don't have your system set to automatically download email for all your accounts. If you do this, the entire email will be downloaded rather than only the header. You can get around this problem by using send/receive groups, as discussed in the next section. To check whether you are downloading email automatically, select Tools ➤ Options, switch to the Mail Setup tab, and click Send/Receive. If you still have the default send/receive group configured (All Accounts), then selecting the Schedule an Automatic Send/Receive Every xx Minutes option will download your email automatically for all accounts.

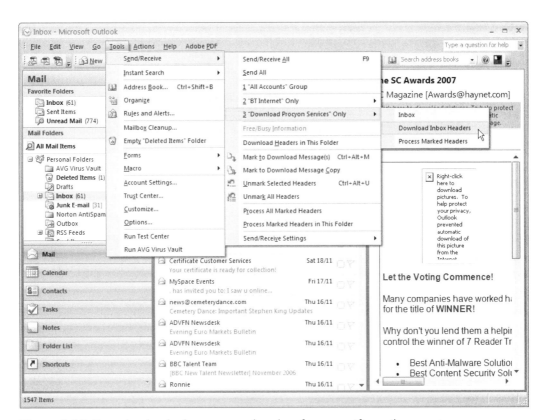

Figure 3-15. Download only the message headers for a specific mail account.

If you are downloading only message headers, you can right-click the message header in your inbox and select what action you'd like taken on that message. For example, if you need to download three emails from the seventeen in your list, right-click each one in turn, and select Mark to Download Message Copy. You can also instruct Outlook to delete messages you don't want to be downloaded or retained on the server by selecting Delete or simply pressing the Delete key after highlighting the message.

When you've finished marking the headers of the messages you'd like to process, it's a simple matter of selecting Tools ➤ Send/Receive "account" Only ➤ Process Marked Headers.

The benefit of using multiple send/receive groups is that you can instruct Outlook to behave differently depending on your situation at the time. If, for example, you usually download your email to your laptop over a broadband connection but when you travel with business you use a dial-up connection from a hotel room, you could configure a special Away From Home send/receive group for the dial-up connection.

> **NOTE** You can use send/receive groups for POP3 accounts but not for HTTP accounts, such as Hotmail (Windows Live Mail), or IMAP accounts.

Setting Up Send/Receive Groups

To set up a new send/receive group in Outlook, do the following:

1. Select Tools ➤ Send/Receive Settings ➤ Define Send/Receive Groups. The Send/Receive Groups dialog box appears (see Figure 3-16).

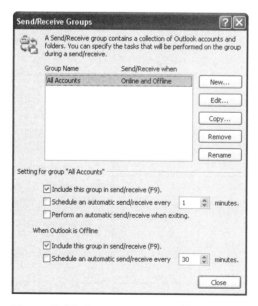

Figure 3-16. Set up a new send/receive group for selective message header processing.

2. Click New, and then give the send/receive group a meaningful name (see Figure 3-17), such as Away. Then click OK.

Figure 3-17. Give the new send/receive group a meaningful name.

3. You'll then see the Send/Receive Settings – Away dialog box. On the left side of the dialog box, select the accounts you intend to process through this send/receive group. To select an account, highlight it on the left side, and then select Include the Selected Account in This Group (see Figure 3-18).

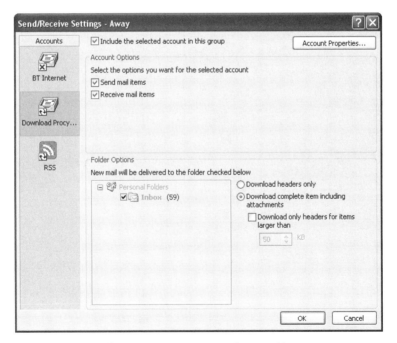

Figure 3-18. Add as many accounts to this send/receive group as you deem necessary.

4. Under the Account Options heading, select whether you want to send mail items or receive mail items; if necessary, you can select both checkboxes for a two-way transfer.

5. Under Folder Options, specify whether to download the headers only or download a complete item including an attachment. Or you can specify a maximum size you will completely download, leaving anything larger than the specified threshold on the server. When you're done, click OK.

You can also instruct Outlook to keep copies of your messages on the POP3 server by selecting Tools ➤ Account Settings. Then highlight the appropriate POP3 account in the list, and then click Change. When you see the Change E-mail Account dialog box, click the More Settings button, and then select the Advanced tab (see Figure 3-19).

Figure 3-19. Configure Outlook to keep a copy of your email on the POP3 server.

This is extremely useful if you have multiple computers that need to access your email; for example, you might have a laptop and a desktop device, and you want your email on both systems, no matter where you are. If you select the checkbox labeled Leave a Copy of Messages on the Server, this will ensure both systems can access the mail. To stop you from having to manually remove items from the server that you've already downloaded to both computers (as in this example), you can have them automatically removed after a period of time (the default being ten days), and you can also ask Outlook to remove all items from the server that have been deleted from your Deleted Items folder.

CHAPTER 4

Contacts and Address Books

One of the most important facets of Outlook is that it manages contacts. In Outlook terms, a *contact* is simply a record of the postal addresses, phone numbers, email addresses, and fax numbers associated with someone with whom you need to keep in touch. For example, you might have personal contacts such as your mother, dentist, and lawyer, and you might have business contacts such as customers, suppliers, and managers.

Contacts can be as detailed or as sparse with information as you require; some may be a simple email address, while others may comprise a complete list of all the ways you can contact the person.

Outlook 2007 contacts are mildly enhanced over previous versions with the inclusion of an editable business card, as shown in Figure 4-1. If you right-click the business card, you have the option of copying the picture to the Clipboard and using it elsewhere, or you can modify the business card layout to better suit your needs (this is covered later).

This chapter introduces you to using Outlook contacts and how these personal information items integrate into the wider Outlook Address Book functionality. In addition, we'll show how to compile your own *distribution lists* (lists of contacts that you can use for bulk-email sending) and how to share distribution lists with other Outlook users.

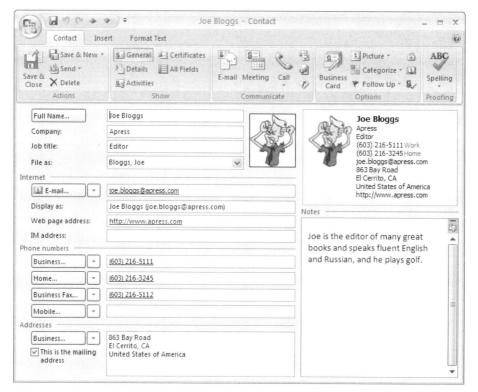

Figure 4-1. The business card adds a new dimension of realism to your contacts.

Using the Contacts Folder

On the left side of the user interface, you'll see a list of the primary functions of Outlook: Mail, Calendar, Contacts, Tasks, and Notes. To access the Contacts folder, you can click Contacts, click Go on the main menu bar, and then select Contacts; alternatively, you can press the keyboard shortcut, Ctrl+3.

You can view and search current contacts in many ways, which we'll cover in a moment, but first we'll show how to create a new contact entry.

Adding a New Contact

The process for adding a new contact from the Contacts interface is as follows:

1. Click New, and then select Contact (or you can press the keyboard shortcut Ctrl+N). This opens a blank contact window (Figure 4-2) where you can start filling in the contact's details.

2. Fill in the details where appropriate, and notice that as you go, the business card is automatically generated for you.

3. If you click the Full Name button, you can add a title, such as Dr., Mr., Mrs., or Prof., and a suffix, such as I, Jr., or Sr.

4. Clicking the E-mail button allows you to search for a particular email in your existing contacts list, and if you click the down arrow to the right of the E-mail button, you can add up to three addresses for this contact.

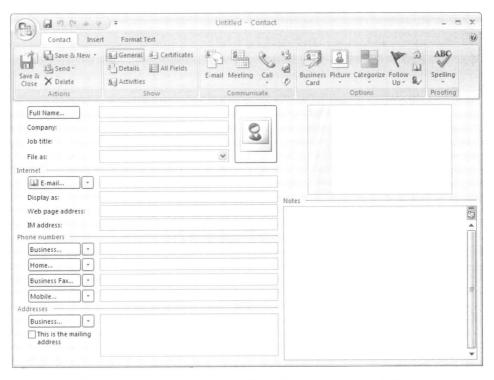

Figure 4-2. To add a contact, type the details in the new contact window, and then click Save.

5. You can record 19 phone number categories in each contact. By clicking the down arrow beside any one of the four phone number labels, you'll see the entire list where you can select to view any four phone numbers at a time. Each phone number can automatically have the appropriate country prefix added, as well as an area code and, if appropriate, an extension number. To add this data, click the phone number label, and fill in the details as required (see Figure 4-3).

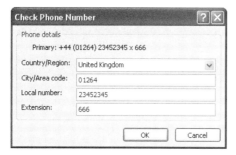

Figure 4-3. Enter additional data for each phone number as required.

6. You have the option of adding a total of three postal addresses (right-click the down arrow next to the address label) for Business, Home, and Other. One of them can be displayed by default in the contact window, while all three are displayed on the business card.

7. To add a photograph, click the icon, and select a picture. This adds the picture to the business card too, so if you're considering this as a proper business card, it might be more appropriate to include a company logo rather than the contact's picture.

8. At the top of the contact window (on the menu bar), you can click Save & Close if you're finished editing.

Creating New Contacts from the Same Company

If you want to create a new contact using the same company details as shown in a previous contact, you can shortcut the process of filling in the company details by highlighting the old contact and selecting Actions ➤ New Contact from Same Company.

This creates a new contact item with all the details intact from the source contact relating to the company, leaving you the quick and easy task of filling in the contact's personal details, such as the name, email address, and IM address.

Using Contacts

Your new contact will be stored in the Contacts folder for future use; however, you should be aware of some advanced contact management facilities, which we'll cover in this section.

Notice on the menu bar, the General view is highlighted. This view is the one you have been working in and contains the business card, address and phone details, Notes area, and contact picture. If you click the Details view, you have the option of adding some further details about the contact, related to the department they work in, their manager's name, their contact's nickname, and, usefully, the address details of an Internet-based free/busy service to determine whether the contact is available.

Clicking the Activities button will show activities associated with that contact, allowing you to track other Outlook items such as tasks that are relevant to this contact.

The Certificates button will display any digital IDs associated with the contact and allow you, if you desire, to import them from an external source.

> **NOTE** You can use digital IDs to securely send information using email, protecting the content's confidentiality and integrity from prying eyes. You can learn more about digital IDs, or purchase one for your own use, at http://www.verisign.com.

The All Fields button offers a data-only view of all the records contained within the contact (see Figure 4-4). You can quickly augment record fields that are editable from this view.

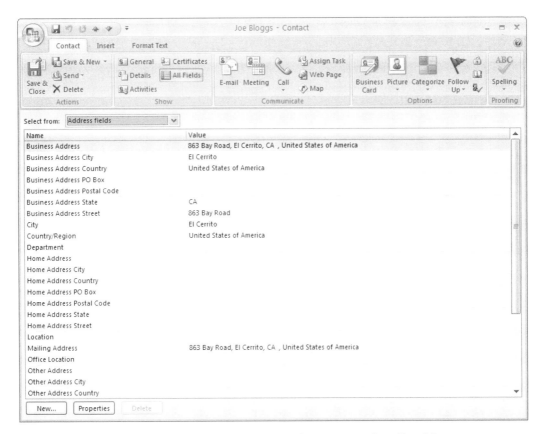

Figure 4-4. Quickly assess and edit your contact information in the All Fields view.

Sending Email and Creating Calendar Appointments

The buttons in the top menu bar in the Communicate group allow you to use this contact to communicate with an external recipient. At the click of a button, you can send an email or set up a calendar appointment with the contact.

The E-mail button creates a new email message, with the To field populated with all the email addresses stored in the contact information.

Clicking the Meeting button instructs Outlook to create a new calendar appointment addressed to all email addresses listed in the contact information.

Phoning a Contact

The Call button is an interesting addition to Outlook; it allows you to make a telephone call to a contact using your computer (as long as you have a modem installed).

This feature uses your system's standard telephony service (typically a modem would be used with a headset) and automatically dials the contact's telephone number using your system's predefined dialing rules, such as external line dialing prefixes (in the case where you might be using a private exchange) and any other special dialing rules that might be required.

When you click the Call button, you see the New Call dialog box shown in Figure 4-5 where you are required to confirm that the phone number details are correct (obtained from the primary phone number in the contact information) and then click Start Call.

Figure 4-5. Calling a contact on the telephone is easy using the contact call feature.

If you click the Dialing Options button in the New Call dialog box, you can add speed-dial numbers (see Figure 4-6). Speed-dial numbers are available from the Call drop-down menu on the main contact page.

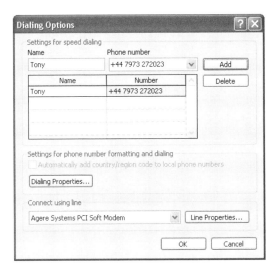

Figure 4-6. Add speed-dial entries to access them directly from the Call menu.

You can also modify the modem dialing properties via this dialog box if required.

Assigning Tasks, Viewing Web Pages, and Locating Addresses

You can assign an Outlook task to a contact, as long as you are allowed to do so by the contact, of course.

> **NOTE** If you are using Exchange Server, you should check with your system administrator about how to set this up. You will need to ensure that the security settings permit one user to assign tasks to another.

To do so, click the Assign Task button, and follow the usual process for creating a task. When you save the task, it is assigned to the contact automatically.

If you click the Web Page button, the Home Page identified in the contact's web address information opens in Internet Explorer.

The final button to discuss in the Communicate group is Map. Clicking Map will use Microsoft's Live Local service powered by Virtual Earth to open a street map focused on the postal address of the contact, as shown in Figure 4-7.

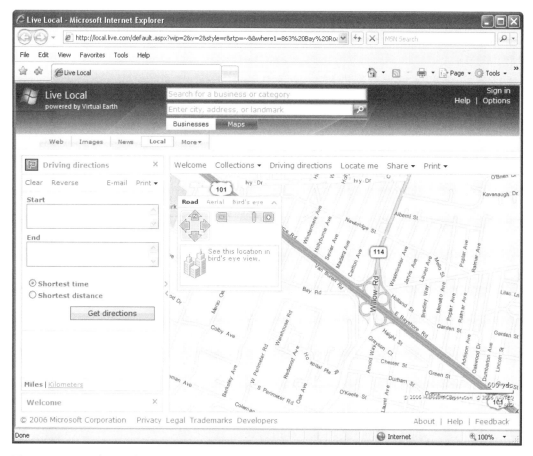

Figure 4-7. Find out where a contact is based using the Live Local service.

Modifying Business Cards

The format of the business card is not set in stone. If you right-click the business card image and select Edit Business Card (or simply click the Business Card button in the top menu bar), you'll see the Edit Business Card dialog box, as shown in Figure 4-8.

From here, you can select a new image if desired and modify the alignment and scaling of the current image. You can also change the layout using any of a series of six predefined patterns, and you can change the background color.

On the left side of the dialog box you'll see the Fields list. Nine fields are already selected to create the business card; however, you have the option of assigning a further seven fields from the information stored within the contact.

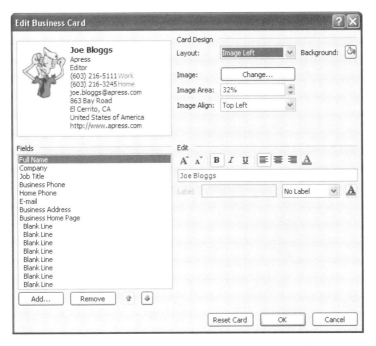

Figure 4-8. Modify the business card to reflect the information you most need at your fingertips.

To add a new field to the business card, highlight one of the empty fields labeled Blank Line, and then click Add. When you see the possible data fields to choose from, select the one you want to be represented on the blank line. It will be automatically added to the list. To move a field up or down, highlight the one in question, and then use the arrow buttons. To remove a field from a business card, highlight the field, and then click Remove. Removing a field changes the entry in the list to Blank Line but does not affect the underlying data stored in the contact.

> **NOTE** You can modify the font size, color, and alignment for each text entry in the field list individually. By default, only the Full Name field is styled differently from the rest; however, it's sometimes worth changing the most used contact information, such as the primary telephone number, to a different color to make it stand out. This all comes down to personal preference.

Viewing Contacts

On the left side of the Contacts folder, you'll notice that eight individual views are listed that rearrange the way your exiting contacts are displayed. Although this is not a new feature of Outlook, a new view that really is worth experimenting with is the Business Card view. The Business Card view will display your contacts as proper business cards in a list that you can scroll through (see Figure 4-9).

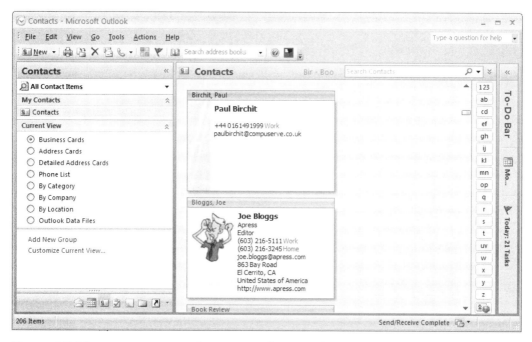

Figure 4-9. View your contacts as business cards to get the convenience of the Rolodex feel.

Customizing the Contacts View

You can change the layout of the Contacts view easily by adding new data fields, grouping data fields, and sorting and filtering data to best suit your requirements.

To change how a view is presented, highlight the view you intend to edit (selecting the appropriate radio button), and then click Customize Current View.

If you find you have adversely affected the presentation of the contact details and want to reset it to how it was when Outlook was installed, click the Reset Current View button.

Adding Contacts from Emails

You can create contact items directly from email you have received in your inbox. To do this, locate the email you are interested in, right-click the email address (in any of the address fields, such as To, CC, or From), and then select Add to Outlook Contacts. This will create a new contact with the email address already filled in.

> **TIP** If you are unsure as to whether a contact item exists for an addressee, you can right-click the email address and select Look Up Outlook Contact. If the addressee exists, the contact opens, and you can edit it as you please. If the contact does not exist, you get an error message stating "Could not find a contact with this e-mail address."

Multiple Contact Folders

It's possible to create multiple contact folders to help you keep yourself organized. You might, for example, want a personal contact folder and a separate one for business. Alternatively, if you deal with a lot of different people in your own organization, you might want to have multiple folders, one for each department.

To create a new contact folder, select File ➤ New ➤ Folder. When you see the Create New Folder dialog box, make sure the Folder Contains drop-down menu says Contact Items and you have highlighted the folder location where you want the new contact folder to appear. You can have it as a top-level folder or have it within a sub-folder—the choice depends on how you want to organize your information. When you're done, click OK.

Sharing Contacts with Other Users

Two options exist for sharing a contact with another user. If you highlight the contact you want to share and then click the Actions button, you'll see two menu items:

- Send As Business Card
- Send Full Contact

If you Send As Business Card, the contact is attached to an email as a vCard, as shown in Figure 4-10, and the image of the business card is embedded in the email body. If you select Send Full Contact, you'll see two further options: In Internet Format (vCard) and In Outlook Format. Selecting In Internet Format (vCard) will send the contact as a vCard but does not include a picture of the business card. Selecting In Outlook Format sends the contact to another Outlook user to import into her own Contacts folder.

> **NOTE** The vCard format is widely accepted by other email systems and will allow you to transfer contact details across multiple platforms. vCard files have the .vcf file extension and automatically open in Outlook if double-clicked.

If you receive an email that has a contact included as an attachment, it's a simple matter of double-clicking it, amending it if necessary, and then clicking Save & Close.

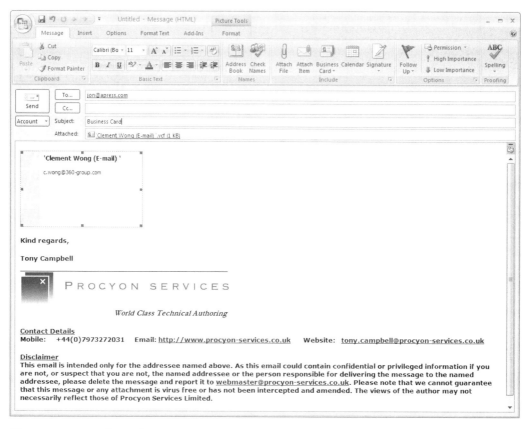

Figure 4-10. Sending a business card attaches both a vCard and an image to your email.

Working with Address Books

In addition to the Contacts folder you've already examined, another view of addresses is available, known as the Address Book.

> **NOTE** The Outlook Address Book opens when you click To, CC, or BCC when you are constructing a new email.

The significance of the Address Book over and above what you can do with your Contacts folder is not immediately apparent, so we'll take a little tour around the bigger picture of address management to put both contacts and the Address Book into context.

First, you should realize that Outlook contacts are merely one of a variety of forms of address that you can store. You can have multiple address books, each with its own folder for your contacts within it, and you can create distribution lists of addresses, based on both contacts and addresses in other address books.

Second, it's important to understand that you manage the big picture with regards to contacts through the Address Book, with the Contacts folder being just one of the many sources for addresses within Outlook.

To access the Address Book (see Figure 4-11), select Tools ➤ Address Book.

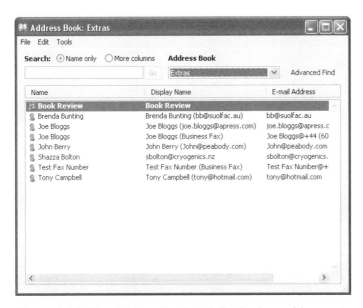

Figure 4-11. The Address Book initially displays addresses in your Contacts folder.

This default address book is known as the Outlook Address Book (OAB) and is created when you install Outlook even if no email accounts have been configured. By default, the OAB contacts only one folder: Contacts.

We described adding contact folders to Outlook earlier, and you have the choice of adding them to the OAB or not. Try to think of the OAB as a consolidator of address books and contact folders. Therefore, you should treat it more as a contact-viewing mechanism than as a discrete container.

In addition to the OAB, you can also have a Mobile Address Book (MAB) attached to an Outlook profile. The MAB is a separate entity from the OAB, with the information within being independent from the information in your contacts so you can store contact information that you need to take with you when you are away from home or the office.

You can also connect Outlook to a third-party Lightweight Directory Access Protocol (LDAP) directory service if one Address Book exists in your environment. Your administrator will give you the appropriate server name and login details for connecting to the LDAP service.

Lastly, if you are hooked into an Exchange server, addresses will be served from there to your Outlook client by your Exchange administrator. This will provide you with a third kind of address book known as a Global Address List (GAL). The GAL is flexible and allows the Exchange administrator to provide corporate information in a variety of ways; however, as an Outlook user, you have no control over what you see in the GAL. Instead, this is solely in the hands of the administration gods. To change a contact or update a view in the GAL, you'll have to plead with your IT department.

Adding a Mobile Address Book

To add a MAB to your Outlook profile, select Tools ➤ Account Settings. When you see the Account Settings dialog box, select the Address Books tab, and then click New. On the Directory or Address Book Type page, select Additional Address Books, then select Mobile Address Book, and then click Next (see Figure 4-12).

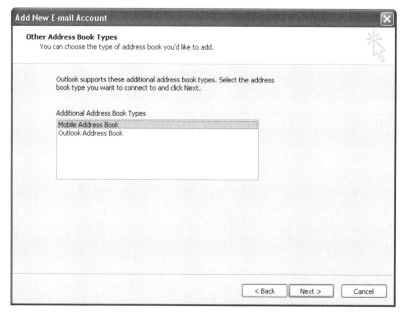

Figure 4-12. Add a MAB to synchronize with a Windows Mobile device.

> **TIP** You can have only one MAB associated with any single Outlook profile at a time. You are not allowed to add MABs through the interface. To have a separate MAB, you need to create a new Outlook profile.

Configuring the Address Book

Frankly, you can do little configuration with the OAB; customization is limited to controlling the order in which the items are presented:

- First Last (John Smith)
- File As (Smith, John)

To toggle between these options, you should open the Account Settings dialog box (Tools ➤ Account Settings), switch to the Address Books tab, highlight the Outlook Address Book, and select Change. You'll see the Microsoft Office Outlook Address Book, as shown in Figure 4-13. Select the way you'd like your contacts displayed, and then click Close.

Figure 4-13. Toggle the way contacts are displayed in the OAB.

Creating Distribution Lists

Sometimes you'll inevitably need to send an email to multiple recipients. If that same group of recipients (for instance, team members in your project team or your drinking buddies) in the future will be receiving more emails from you, you should consider setting them up in what's called a *distribution list*.

Just like individual contacts, distribution lists are contained within the Outlook Address Book and can be addressed from a new email simply by clicking To, CC, or BCC. The only difference between a contact and a distribution list is that a distribution list is a container that can hold contacts and other distribution lists.

TIP When you send an email using a distribution list, the list can appear in the To, CC, or BCC field of the email. If you add the distribution list to the To field or the CC field, all addressees in the distribution list will be able to see everyone else's address. If you prefer to keep addressees' details anonymous from each other, send the email with the distribution list in the BCC field. This way, all email addresses remain private.

It's really easy to set up a distribution list; the following procedure should get you up and running in no time:

1. Select Tools ➤ Address Book.

2. Select File ➤ New Entry.

3. In the New Entry dialog box, highlight New Distribution List. Make sure you select the folder you want the distribution list to be created in at the bottom of the screen (see Figure 4-14) before you proceed by clicking OK.

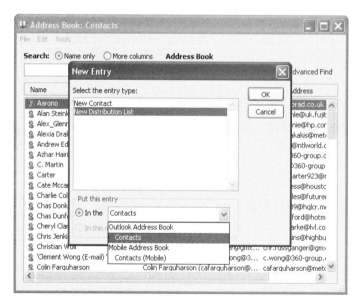

Figure 4-14. Make sure you select the contact folder in which you want the distribution list to be stored.

4. The Untitled – Distribution List dialog box appears, with no items yet selected in the list. Try to give the distribution list a meaningful name so when you see the one-line title in the Address Book, you know what its purpose is.

5. To add existing contacts to the distribution list, click the Select Members button at the top of the dialog box to pick contacts from the Address Book. Contacts will appear in the dialog box, as shown in Figure 4-15.

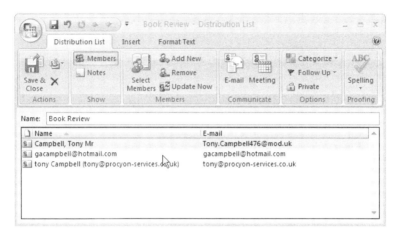

Figure 4-15. Recipients will be listed in the Details pane of the distribution list.

6. If you want to add contact information to this distribution list not already in your Address Book, click the Add New button, and type the recipient's name and email address in the dialog box provided.

7. When you've added all the contact details you require to your distribution list, click Save & Close.

You can add an in-depth description to a distribution list by clicking the Notes button on the Ribbon at the top of the screen (in the Show group). If you click the Send button (the small icon next to the Save & Close button), you can forward the distribution list as an email attachment to someone else for their own use.

TIP To add a distribution list, you receive in an email to your own Address Book, double-click it to open it, edit it if necessary, and then click Save & Close.

CHAPTER 5

Calendaring

Scheduling your busy life can be a chore, and you don't want to have to fight your software to do it. Outlook 2007 includes some minor, but welcome, improvements to its Calendar module, with particular emphasis on sharing calendars with your co-workers and associates through Exchange Server, through Office Online, and through the Internet.

In this chapter, we cover how the calendar works; how to schedule appointments, meetings, and events; how to share your calendar information in a variety of ways; how to integrate SharePoint with the Outlook Calendar; and how to customize your calendar to fit your work style. We round out the chapter with some tips on getting the most from the calendar.

Understanding the Logic of the Calendar Structure

People generally think their calendar, daybook, or appointment book is the most personal organizational tool they own. Although users might be agnostic about email or task management, they almost always already have a system in place for managing when and where they need to be at certain times through the day. Paper calendars are still a multibillion-dollar industry in the United States. Electronically managing time is a phenomenon that will not happen overnight.

Part of the reason many people still keep paper appointment registers is because the electronic tools that exist to date aren't easy to use. Sure, pointing and clicking and typing in a GUI calendar is simple, but what happens when you're out of the office and need an update about where you're supposed to be? If you don't have a PDA and you didn't have the foresight to print a copy of your daily scheduling, you're out of luck; the paper user, on the other hand, always has the most updated copy of his schedule with him. The "master schedule problem" is not easy to solve, short of everyone making a run on PDAs at the local electronics store.

Although that problem will continue to exist, electronic timekeeping typically had other difficulties in the past, as follows:

- It wasn't easy to quickly look at a calendar and see what was happening on a given day, week, or month. Entries looked the same, highlighting wasn't possible, times weren't consistently displayed, and so on.

- Sharing electronic calendars was a pain. With a paper book, you and a colleague can quickly determine what times are available for a short meeting; with an electronic calendar, often several emails were required to finalize a time and place for a meeting, since viewing each person's calendars was quite difficult.

- There was no interaction, integration, and relationship between electronic task management programs and electronic calendar programs. The two just didn't talk to one another; even Outlook, which supported both types of data and views, did a horrible job of letting calendar entries and task entries work together for you.

- Meetings on an electronic calendar were nearly impossible to coordinate for a long time. It's still not as easy as it should be.

Outlook 2007 addresses each of these problems in innovative ways, as you will see in this chapter.

Entering and Managing Calendar Data

It is trivially easy to get started using the calendar: unlike in previous versions of Outlook, you can simply click any time slot in any view of the calendar and start typing. Outlook creates an entry directly from the main view, eliminating the need to enter data in a separate window. To create a custom entry, you can right-click anywhere in the window and choose from any of the options presented.

Creating a standard appointment is easy—just right-click the calendar anywhere, and select New Appointment. If you target your clicking to a certain time slot, the appointment window will open with that time preselected. Figure 5-1 shows the appointment window.

The Ribbon contains controls that allow you to adjust the context of this appointment. Use the Show As command to classify the meeting as busy, out-of-office time, or something else—this is useful if you share your calendar with others, a process covered later in this chapter in the "Sharing Your Calendar with Others" section.

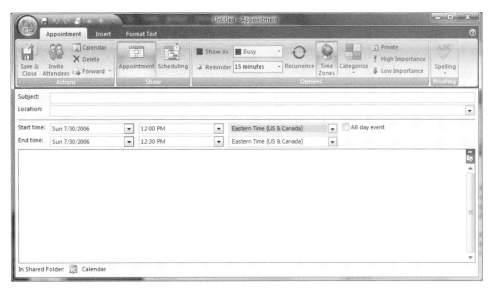

Figure 5-1. The appointment window

A useful addition is the time zones feature, which allows you to control the time zone of meetings and appointments from directly within the data window. For example, imagine that you work in New York but often schedule conference calls with colleagues in your United Kingdom office. Your colleague in the United Kingdom wants to set up a conference call at 3 p.m. his time. Here, you can simply set the meeting up for 3 p.m. and, from the time zone drop-down box beside the start and end time, choose the target time zone. Your calendar automatically adjusts to your time zone, and if you're using a meeting request, his calendar will adjust as well, so everyone is in sync without doing crazy time math in your head.

In addition, inviting people to meetings is easier with Outlook 2007 than with previous versions—Outlook has always done a pretty good job of coordinating people's schedules, finding times for a particular meeting given certain constraints, and managing the attendee list in the days prior to an event. However, the workflow of the automated meeting messages was a bit hairy in some situations: there could be multiple updates to a meeting, each triggering an email that you would then have to manually accept or decline. In Outlook 2007, meeting attendees do not have to continually accept minor meeting updates when you originally accept a meeting the first time; however, important changes, such as a modification to the meeting time, date, or location, will still require your intervention.

To create a new meeting, right-click the calendar (anywhere), select New Meeting Request, and then click the Scheduling button on the Ribbon. You'll see a screen like Figure 5-2.

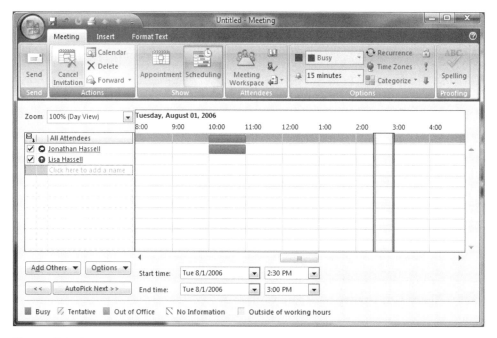

Figure 5-2. Setting up a new meeting request

You can add attendees to the meeting request by typing their names in the list. If you are using Microsoft Exchange, Exchange will grab their calendar data and show blocks of time the other meeting attendees have already committed. If your list gets too long to easily reconcile free time visually, you can use the AutoPick option by clicking the AutoPick Next button at the bottom of the screen. Scrolling left or right in the scheduling window navigates through the days of the week; only the default work times are displayed, eliminating evenings, early mornings, and weekends.

If you click the Meeting Workspace button on the Ribbon, you can create a SharePoint-based workspace to store documents, tasks, and premeeting discussion threads in a central place. (You'll learn more about SharePoint a bit later in the "Connecting SharePoint Calendars to Outlook" section.) You can also adjust for time zones for the individual meeting attendees by clicking the Time Zones button, or you can set a recurring appointment by clicking the Recurrence button.

Categorizing

Previously, you could categorize calendar items, contacts, and tasks, but only calendar items were color coded, and there wasn't an easy (or even complex but intuitive) method to sort items in various views by category, which led a majority of users to wonder what sort of return on their time investment they would receive by even starting to categorize their Outlook items. And indeed, there wasn't much. However, the approach to categorizing in Outlook 2007 has changed—now you can assign a category to every common Outlook object, including mail messages, calendar entries, contacts, task items, and notes, and you can further color-code it. The idea is that you can categorize your tasks by project, assigning green, for example, to all mail messages, calendar items, tasks, and quick notes that relate to the same overall set of objectives.

Searching

The instant search feature in Outlook works in the calendar, too. The Search box is located at the top of the Calendar view, whether you're looking at a single day, whole week, or whole month, as shown in Figure 5-3.

Figure 5-3. Calendar instant search

With instant search, you can find categorized mailbox items. To search on a category, just click the chevron to expose more features. You can enter any keywords you like, but to filter search results on just certain categories, click the drop-down list to select the appropriate category. You can see this process in Figure 5-4.

Figure 5-4. Searching for categorized items

You can also search through all categories and look for hits based on keywords in the body or subject line; the location of the meeting, appointment, or event; and the organizer of the meeting. You can see in Figure 5-4 the appropriate places to enter these criteria.

Sharing Your Calendar with Others

Calendars are great for keeping track of your own time, but with Outlook they're great for keeping track of other people's time, too. You have many options for saving, sharing, and publishing calendar data among friends, co-workers, and associates outside your business, using either the built-in groupware functionality of Microsoft Exchange Server or the standard Internet calendar formats and Office Online.

In the following sections, we'll show you some of the ways you can share your appointment, meeting, and event schedules with others automatically using Outlook 2007.

Sharing via Microsoft Exchange Server

If your company uses Microsoft Exchange Server as its groupware solution, then you can use the built-in Exchange Server/Outlook functionality relationship to seamlessly share calendar data between you and other users. Your administrator can give you permission directly to access someone else's calendar, which can be useful if you're managing a subordinate's (or superior's) schedule. Alternatively, if you're a member of an ad hoc team and the members want to share their calendars with each other without involving the IT department, here's how to do it:

1. Navigate to the calendar you want to share.
2. Click the Share My Calendar link in the left pane of the window.
3. A new message window appears, with details about your request, as shown in Figure 5-5. You send this message to the person with whom you want to share your calendar entries. Here you can ask for reciprocal access as well. Enter a note if you want, and click Send.

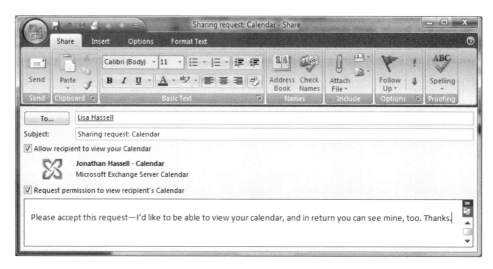

Figure 5-5. Inviting someone to see your shared calendar

4. Outlook will prompt you to confirm that the recipient should be able to view your calendar. By default, the recipient has only read access to your calendar; in other words, she can't make or change entries. Confirm the request by clicking OK.

Your calendar is now shared. You can verify this by looking for the servant's hand icon (the typical Windows sharing icon) on the Calendar icon in Outlook.

If the recipient grants your request for reciprocal access, you'll receive an email to that effect. In the meantime, if you want to open a calendar that was already shared, click the Open Shared Calendar link, and enter the username of the person whose calendar you want to see. The shared calendar will open, shaded in a different color, aside your default calendar, as shown in Figure 5-6.

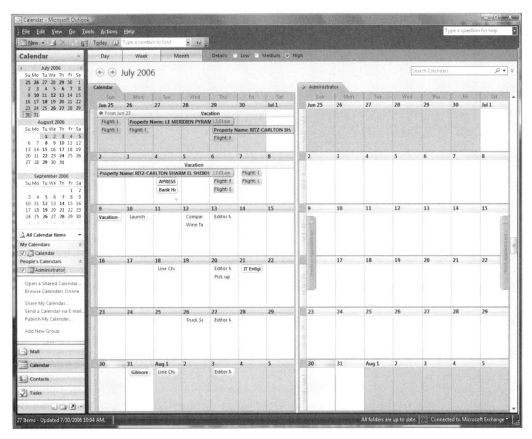

Figure 5-6. The default calendar and a shared calendar, viewed side by side by default

One of the more useful features of Outlook 2007 is the ability to look at shared calendars in overlay mode, which saves you the trouble of lining up days horizontally and looking for time conflicts. The top layer of the calendar is in regular type, and the other layers are always in a darker gray or otherwise identified as being on another calendar, as shown in Figure 5-7. You can click the arrows beside the names of the calendars to go into overlay mode; click the tabs at the top of the window to switch between the calendars and active layers.

Figure 5-7. The default calendar and a shared calendar, viewed overlaid

Sending via Email

If you just want to send your schedule to someone who is outside your organization and you don't want to spend a lot of time writing the times you're available (or not available), sending your calendar via email is a great way to do it. Outlook will take a specific date range, put in as little or as much detail as you want, and put the data in a nice HTML format in the body of a message. Figure 5-8 shows an example of the format.

Sending via email is easy: navigate to the calendar you want to send, and click Send a Calendar via E-mail. A dialog box pops up, asking you to specify the calendar to send, the date range, and the level of detail. Adjust the properties as needed, and click OK. A new message window pops up, with the calendar data both in the body of the email and encoded as an ICS attachment that the recipient can import into his calendar. To import that ICS file, just double-click, and select Open; the related events will automatically be inserted into the default calendar in the user's mailbox.

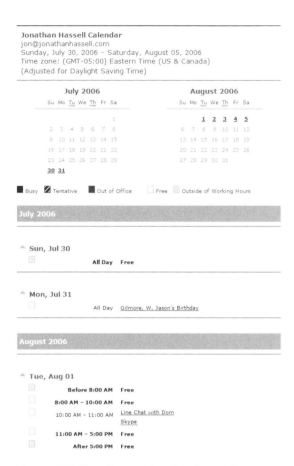

Figure 5-8. Sending a calendar via email

Publishing to Office Online

Microsoft Office Online will host Office application–based data for others to view, manage, and change—with your permission, of course. In the context of calendaring, publishing Outlook Calendars to Office Online is a great way to replicate some of the basic features of Exchange Server calendar sharing without laying out the significant financial investment for Exchange Server. Users within your organization can upload copies of their calendars to Office Online, set those copies to update themselves automatically, and then invite the entire organization or just their division or teammates to look at their calendars online. Although you can't open these calendars directly in Outlook and you can't overlay them or use them in Outlook, you can still get the most up-to-date data about your team by publishing your calendar to Office Online.

To publish your calendar to Office Online, follow these steps:

1. Navigate to the calendar to publish.

2. Click the Publish My Calendar link in the left pane.

3. The Microsoft Office Online Registration page appears. Publishing a calendar to Office Online requires a valid account; these accounts are free, but you need to register for them. You have to register only the first time you use the service. Complete the registration.

4. The Publish Calendar to Microsoft Office Online dialog box appears, as shown in Figure 5-9. Choose the date range to publish, the level of detail, whether to make your calendar details public, and whether to automatically update the online copy of the calendar periodically. As for the level of detail, you can choose to show only parts of your day that you've blocked (without showing the details of the appointments, meetings, or events), limited details (which shows just the time and the subject line of the calendar items), or full details. Once you've made your selections, click OK.

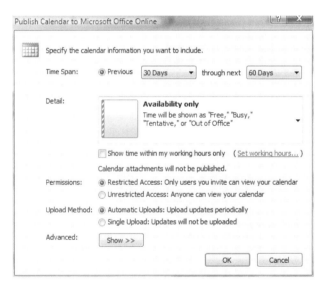

Figure 5-9. The Publish Calendar to Microsoft Office Online dialog box

5. The upload process commences. Once the process is finished, a prompt asks you whether you want to invite people to see your online calendar. Click Yes to proceed with the invitation.

6. A new message window appears, with details of your calendar and a link to the online version of it (note these details in Figure 5-10). Enter the recipients' email addresses. To see your calendar on Office Online, each potential viewee will need to have a valid Windows Live ID registered to the email address you're using in the invitation message. Click Send to transmit the message.

Figure 5-10. Inviting someone to see your published calendar

The process is then complete, and your calendar is published in Microsoft Office Online.

Saving and Subscribing to Internet Calendars

If you have a private web server you'd like to use to share calendars on the Internet, Outlook 2007 supports using it, with a couple of exceptions: first, the only method to restrict access to the calendars you publish is to adjust the file permissions on the target web server, and second, the target web server must support the WebDAV protocol. (The quickest way to find out whether WebDAV is supported is to ask your network administrator; there is no rapid test to see whether it's enabled on a machine.)

Connecting SharePoint Calendars to Outlook

Many corporations are using SharePoint technologies to facilitate team collaboration, scheduling, and document storage. However, Outlook has previously had clunky calendar integration with SharePoint. Outlook 2007 tries to resolve this issue, in conjunction with the latest version of the SharePoint products and technologies.

Here is the official party line from Microsoft about what you can do when integrating the various versions of SharePoint with Outlook 2007:

- You can update your SharePoint calendar by using Outlook if your calendar is on a site that is running Windows SharePoint Services version 3 or Microsoft Office SharePoint Server (MOSS) 2007.

- If you have Windows SharePoint Services 2.0, you can view your SharePoint calendar in Outlook and view it side by side with your Outlook calendars, but you can't update it by using Office Outlook 2007.

You can connect a Windows SharePoint Services calendar to Outlook by logging on to the WSS site and navigating to the target calendar. From the Actions menu, select Connect to Outlook. You'll need to acknowledge the prompt (if given) that Outlook wants access to the Internet, and then the prompt in Figure 5-11 displays. Click OK to finish the connection. You'll see the SharePoint calendar under the Other

Calendars group on the left side of the Outlook window. If the checkboxes are selected for the SharePoint calendar and your default Outlook Calendar, both calendars appear together side by side, or you can overlay them as discussed earlier in this chapter.

Figure 5-11. Connecting a SharePoint calendar to Outlook 2007

You can use the SharePoint calendar just as you would the default personal calendar in Outlook. The SharePoint site will be kept up-to-date as necessary, with one exception: if you modify a meeting request after adding it to a SharePoint-based calendar, the meeting attendees do not automatically receive updates. You'll need to get in touch with the attendees yourself and tell them about the new information. To work around this, add the meeting request to your Outlook Calendar, which will then allow you to send updates as you'd expect.

Customizing the Calendar

You don't have to live with the calendar as it comes out of the box. In the next sections, we'll show some ways to personalize your Outlook Calendar and make it fit your style of work.

Personalizing the Display

You can change some features about how you schedule your time within Outlook's various calendar views. Here are some quick tips:

Change the time scale: The calendar shows 30-minute blocks by default. If you want greater or smaller intervals, right-click any blank area in the calendar, and choose Other Settings. In the Time Scale list, under Day, click the interval you'd like to use, and click OK.

Show week numbers: You can see the number of weeks when using the Month view. Select Tools ➤ Options, then click the Calendar Options button (Figure 5-12 shows it), and check Show Week Numbers in the Month View and Date Navigator.

Set work-time options: If your work week isn't Monday through Friday, your workday isn't 9–5, or your work year doesn't run alongside the calendar year, you can make Outlook's default views match your situation. Select Tools ➤ Options, click Calendar Options (see Figure 5-12), and adjust the defaults from there.

Add or remove a second time zone: If you work with colleagues in multiple locations around the globe, scheduling meetings at a synchronized time can be challenging. Outlook can help by displaying the current time in other time zones alongside your current time for easy viewings. Select Tools ➤ Options, click Calendar Options (see Figure 5-12), and then Time Zone. Check the Show an Additional Time Zone box, type a name for it, and then click the zone you want to add. Click OK.

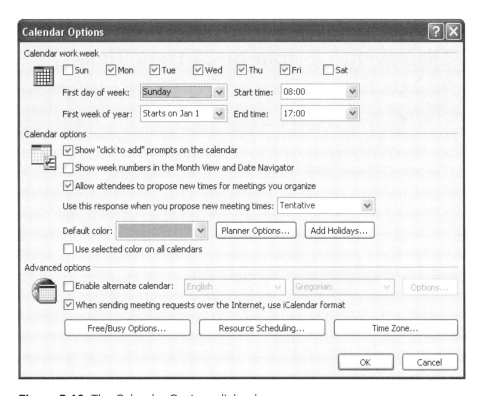

Figure 5-12. The Calendar Options dialog box

Adding Holidays and Events

Outlook ships with a default set of events (essentially appointments without fixed times) so you don't have to manually add them. The events are divided into regions of observation. To add them, select Tools ➤ Options, and then click the Calendar Options button. Click Add Holidays, select your region, and then click OK.

You may want to add custom holidays to a file to distribute to all Outlook users in your company, containing official company days off, paydays, open enrollment for benefits, or other key dates. Here's how: open `C:\Program Files\Microsoft Office\Office 12\LCID\outlook.hol` after first making a safe copy of it somewhere else. Go to the end of the file, and add events using the following format:

```
[Description of Section] nnn
Event or holiday description, yyyy/mm/dd
Event or holiday description, yyyy/mm/dd
```

The `nnn` part represents the number of events within the section. Enter a useful description of the section, and then type the name of the events and the date for each event in the proper format. Save the file, and open Outlook; the new events will import automatically when you execute the previous procedure.

You can distribute the new holiday file, if it would be useful to others, either by emailing it to users or by placing it on a network share. On the target system, the file needs to be put in `C:\Program Files\Microsoft Office\Office 12\LCID\outlook.hol`.

Displaying 12-Hour or 24-Hour Time

The time displayed in the calendar matches the customary display—either 12:mm or 24:mm—of the region in which the operating system thinks it is operating. You can change this, but you change it through the operating system, meaning the modification will affect all applications on your system. In any version of Windows, double-click the clock on the taskbar. Click Regional and Language Options, click Customize, click the Time tab, and then change the time format as appropriate.

CHAPTER 6

Notes and Journals

It's not always possible to produce immediately structured and targeted actions based on information you hear in an ad hoc way. For this reason, with notes and the Journal, you can take down notes and maintain daily records using Outlook; both methods are vital in helping you stay organized and on top of what you have to do.

Notes are scraps or jottings you might, for example, take in a meeting or during a phone call, where you need to get a piece of information down quickly into a form where you can act upon it later. Use Outlook notes in the same way as you would a scratch pad next to the telephone. Take notes quickly, disregard unnecessary ones, act on ones that need action, and then delete them when you're done. You should consider notes temporary information storage items and not keep them long-term. Use too many notes, and your life will become disorganized chaos. On the other hand, not using Outlook notes will force you to use a paper-based system for the same purpose.

Outlook's *Journal* is like having your own personal audit trail. Outlook can keep a complete list of everything you do within the Office environment, including tracking which Word documents you edit and which email you've sent (and to whom). You can also program the Journal to keep track of manual events such as phone calls, meetings, and other scheduled events through its manual item-entry interface.

Working with Notes

You can create a note any time (from any screen) in Outlook by pressing Ctrl+Shift+N. You can also create a new note within the note window by clicking the Notes button in the Navigation pane and then selecting New.

Each note you create is time stamped with the time and date it was created, as shown in Figure 6-1.

Figure 6-1. Creating a new note in
Outlook is extremely straightforward.

By default, Notes are created in a standard size, but you can configure notes to automatically start out life bigger than this through the note options (more about that in a minute), or you can drag the chevron in the bottom-right corner to make an individual note bigger or smaller depending on your needs.

When you have finished typing a note, close it using the Close button in the top-right corner; Outlook will automatically save it, as shown in Figure 6-2.

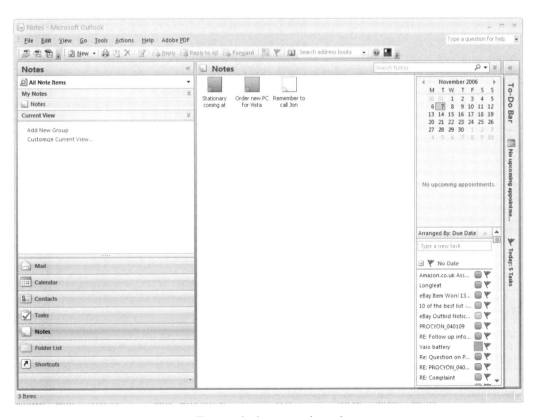

Figure 6-2. Notes are automatically saved when you close them.

Customizing Notes

There's not a lot you can customize in a note; however, you should pay attention to a couple of options. Selecting Tools ➤ Options ➤ Note Options opens the Notes Options dialog box, shown in Figure 6-3.

You can change three aspects about default notes:

- Color
- Size
- Font

You can select, using the Color drop-down menu, the color of the default note (applied when you press Ctrl+Shift+N) from five colors: blue, green, pink, yellow, and white. The default color is yellow (just like the Post-it it was obviously based on).

You can ask Outlook to use three sizes when creating a new note: small, medium, and large. Medium is the default.

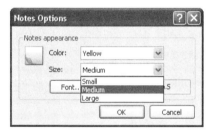

Figure 6-3. You can't customize much about notes other than aesthetic features.

> **TIP** Each time you create a note, irrespective of the default size it is created with, you can drag the window to be as large or small as you please.

You can change the font, font style, and font size used in your notes by clicking the Font button and selecting the appropriate settings from the Font dialog box.

Using Notes

Notes are a temporary storage location for information you have yet to fully process and act upon. This section shows you how to use your notes to create workflow-oriented items such as email messages, calendar appointments, and contacts from your scribbling.

You have two ways to send the contents of a note by email; first, if you drag a note from the notes window onto the Mail button in the Navigation pane, Outlook will create a new email message with the contents of the note in the email body, as shown in Figure 6-4. The subject of the email will be the first line of text from the note, and the entire contents of the note will appear in the message body.

> **CAUTION** Remember to use carriage returns after each line of your note, especially if you are planning to use them as the basis for an email. The carriage return will ensure only the top line of the note, and not a long string of text, becomes the message subject.

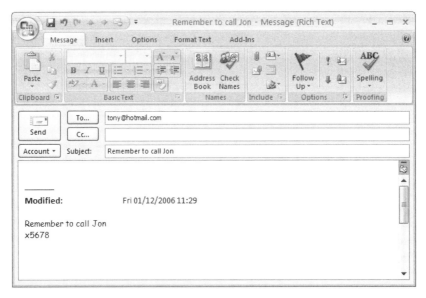

Figure 6-4. The message subject is generated from the first full line of text within the note.

The second method for sending a note to another user is to email it as an attachment. In this way, it remains in the format of an Outlook note and can be opened and used in this context at the other end. To send a note as an attachment, right-click the note in question, and then select Forward.

If you receive a note from someone else, double-click it, edit it if necessary, and then click the Close button to save it to your Notes folder.

If you want to use a note as the basis of a new calendar appointment, drag it onto the Calendar button in the Navigation pane, and amend the new entry as required. In the same way as the email subject was automatically generated from the first line of text within the note, the subject of the calendar appointment is also generated from this text, as shown in Figure 6-5.

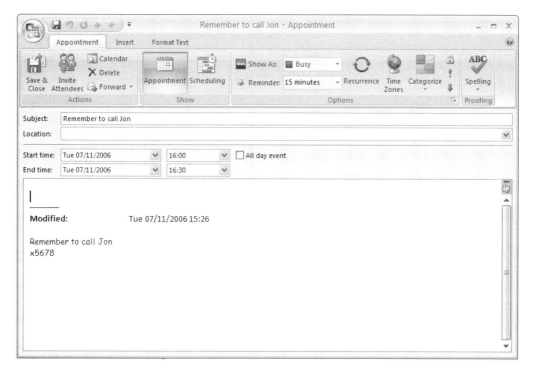

Figure 6-5. Create a calendar appointment based on the content of a note.

You will need to add a location for the meeting, set the start and end times, and also invite any attendees you want to be present. The note will be passed into the appointment message body in the same way as it was for an email.

If a note contains someone's contact details, drag the note to the Contact button in the Navigation pane to create a new contact from the information within. The contents of the note will appear in the Notes section of the new contact, as shown in Figure 6-6. You'll still be required to type all the usual address and contact details for the addressee before the contact is of any use.

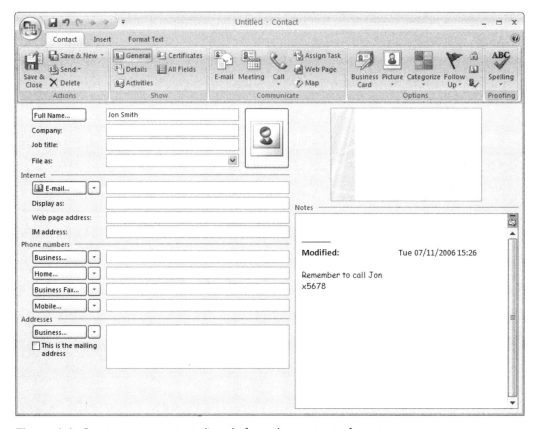

Figure 6-6. Create a new contact directly from the content of a note.

Finally, to create a new task based on the contents of a note, drag the appropriate note onto the Tasks button in the Navigation pane. This will create a new task with the subject of the task taken from the first line of text in the note and the entire note pasted into the task body.

Assigning Contacts to Notes

You can quickly assign Address Book contacts to individual notes, effectively marking them as information related to that contact. This can be useful (although somewhat limited since there's nothing much you can do with them) because any contact assigned to a note will appear as plain text in an email or a new personal contact. In this way, you can quickly record the person the note was related to, although you could probably type this information into the note as it would take to locate it in the Address Book.

To assign a contact, click the note's menu button (at the top left of the note), and then select Contacts from the menu. Click the Contacts button in the Contacts for Note dialog box, and then select all the relevant contact names from the Address Book.

Assigning Categories to Notes

Color categories are extremely useful throughout Outlook, and note-taking is no exception. To assign a color category to a note, simply highlight the appropriate note, click the Color Category icon on the toolbar, and select the appropriate category from the list.

Alternately, while you are creating or editing a note, click the Note menu button (at the top left of the note), then click Categorize, and finally select the appropriate category from the list (see Figure 6-7).

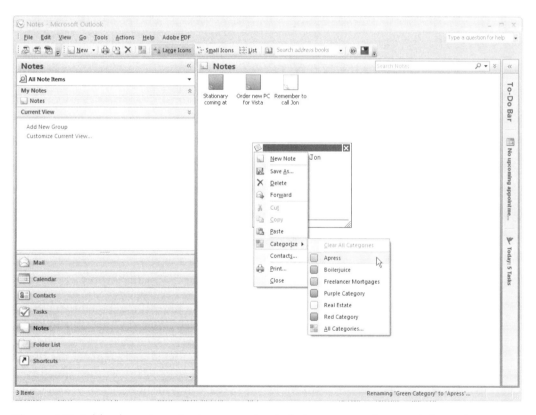

Figure 6-7. Add color categories to your notes to help you organize your information.

Working with the Journal

You should think of the Journal as your electronic audit trail, recording everything you do within the Office environment for future reference. For example, to keep track of all the activities that related to writing this book, we used the Journal to record the time spent writing and editing each chapter, the time it took to send emails back and forth to Apress, and the time spent outside of the automatically monitored environment, such as reading and researching. When we analyze this information, we can quickly see how much effort a particular work stream took.

The Journal can collect information about the following items:

- Email messages
- Meeting requests
- Meeting cancellations
- Meeting responses
- Task requests
- Task responses
- Files from Office Access
- Files from Office Excel
- Files from Office PowerPoint
- Files from Office Visio
- Files from Office Word

You can configure the Journal to record a wide variety of items, and in each case you can specify which Address Book contacts you should be collecting Journal entries for. In this way, communications with work-related contacts may be recorded, while personal emails and appointments are ignored.

Configuring the Journal

To configure the Journal, you'll need to switch on the Journal functionality by selecting Tools ➤ Options; then on the Preferences tab, select Journal Options. This opens the Journal Options dialog box, as shown in Figure 6-8.

Start by selecting the items you'd like recorded in your Journal using the checkboxes in the top-left corner. You can specify individual contacts on the right side of the screen; this is useful for recording items that are important rather than everything that happens—in auditing terms, information overload is almost as bad as not auditing at all. Also, you can instruct the Journal to record information pertaining to other Office applications, such as Word and PowerPoint, so you can get a much clearer picture of what you've been doing.

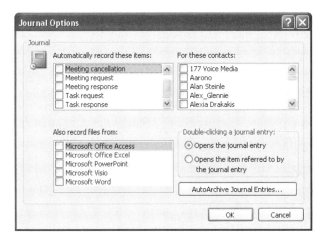

Figure 6-8. Switch on the Journal from specific items and contacts.

Notice that Outlook can take one of two actions when a Journal entry is double-clicked:

- It can open the Journal entry.
- It can open the item referred to by the Journal entry.

The former of the two options will open a dialog box containing all the information about a specific Journal entry, such as the time, date, to whom a message was sent, and so on. The second option will open the item in question, so instead of seeing the metadata associated with the item, you see the item itself.

> **CAUTION** It's a good idea to keep Opens the Journal Entry as the default action if you double-click a Journal entry. This way, you give yourself the option to open the embedded item after assessing the content of the Journal item. Remember, Journal items might contain viruses or other such malicious code.

We'll cover the AutoArchive settings a little later, but for now, we'll talk about the Journal itself. Click OK when you're ready.

Using the Journal Interface

You access the Journal from the Go menu by selecting Journal, or you can press Ctrl+8. When you first enter the Journal, you'll be asked whether you want to switch it on. Select Yes to begin.

The Journal looks like Figure 6-9. Notice that the horizontal scroll bar along the bottom of the window will scroll back and forward through time, with each entry recorded against the date and time it happened.

CAUTION The Journal adds processing overhead to your system that could be detrimental to your Office experience. If you find that your system suddenly starts running really slowly, try turning off the Journal or recording less information to see whether that helps.

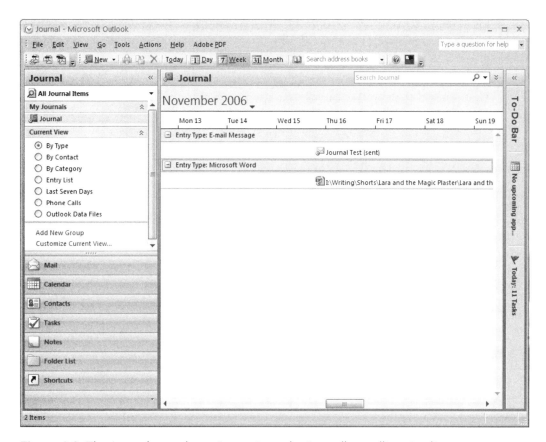

Figure 6-9. The Journal records entries against a horizontally scrolling timeline.

As events occur that match your Journal settings, such as your sending an email or opening a Word document, Outlook will create an entry for that event. The type of Journal event created appears on the left side of the screen, while the contents of the event appear on the right. To open a specific Journal entry, double-click the entry icon.

Recording Journal Entries

A Journal entry looks very much like any other Outlook object. The subject of each Journal entry usually contains the Outlook object subject heading (such as the email subject line or the calendar appointment subject), or it will contain the path to where the Office file being accessed is located, as shown in Figure 6-10.

Figure 6-10. A typical Journal entry will contain either an Outlook item or another Office file.

When you start the Journal collecting events that occur on your system, it's always there in the background collecting information. It runs a small program in the background of your Office system, and even when Outlook is not active, the Journal will still record access to Office files.

This kind of automatic journaling of information is useful if you want to later scrutinize how you operate your system or distribute your time amongst tasks. You can see how often you communicate with certain individuals, how frequently you edit certain documents, and how regularly you access spreadsheets or databases. This record of your time can help you plan projects in the future as you start to get a better picture of how you operate.

Nevertheless, automatic journaling in isolation has a drawback—you will not be recording events that are outside the control of Office. For example, a 30-minute telephone conversation will not be recorded and may be as important a part of the daily activity plan as some of the automatically recorded events. This is where you can use manual Journal entries to augment the overall picture with events that are outside the control of the Journal system.

To create a manual Journal entry, click the New button in the main Journal window, type the entry subject, and add a time and date. You can also add some notes to enhance the metadata associated with this manual entry. Use the drop-down list to select an entry type, and apply any color categories that fit with this event.

> **TIP** If you are planning a phone call or some other manual Journal entry type, you should create a new entry before you start the phone call; then when you begin, click the Start Timer button at the top of the screen. When you finish the phone call, click Pause Timer. This will record the exact duration of the event in the entry.

Using Journal Views

The Journal has seven distinct views for changing the appearance of the Journal interface:

- By Type
- By Contact
- By Category
- Entry List
- Last Seven Days
- Phone Calls
- Outlook Data Files

The default view for the Journal is By Type, which is the view you've already seen in previous figures. Entries are arranged on a horizontal timeline and are easily accessed by double-clicking the item. You should use the By Type view when you are interested in scrutinizing what events occurred over a specific period of time. This view is not so useful if you are looking for a specific event type or embedded object, such as a particular Word document or Excel spreadsheet.

By Contact will also arrange the entries on a timeline; however, they are not grouped using the contact name associated with an Outlook item.

The By Category view organizes the Journal entries according to the color category associated with each one. You can use this view to arrange the Journal in such a way as to group activities related to a specific project (determined by the preset color category).

The Entry List view removes the reliance on the timeline, instead listing all entries in a table form, as shown in Figure 6-11. This view is extremely useful since you can use the column header in much the same way as you'd arrange files in Windows Explorer to order the entries based on a variety of attributes, such as type, subject, time, and contact.

> **NOTE** The paper-clip icon indicates that an entry has an associated object embedded within it. This might be an attached email, a document, or a spreadsheet. Where there is no paper clip, Outlook has recorded a simple event that has no associated content, or it is associated with a manual event you created with no attachment.

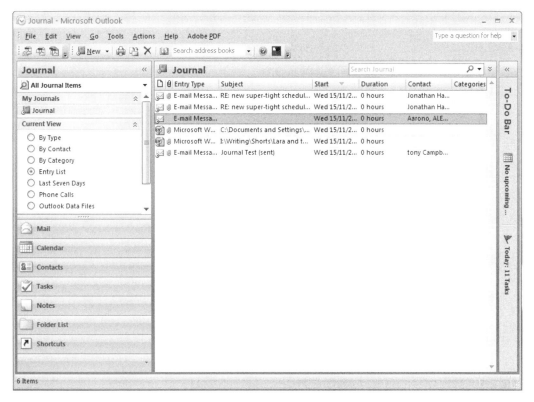

Figure 6-11. Journal entries in the Entry List view are easy to view and sort.

If you switch to the Last Seven Days view, you'll get a similar list to that of the Entry List view; however, Outlook will show you the entries from only the past seven days.

NOTE You can modify any of the views shown here by clicking Customize Current View. Use the Filter button to instruct Outlook to display entries of only a specific type, or use a search phase, such as the project name. You can create more advanced filters, such as the one used in the Last Seven Days view, through the SQL tab in the Filter dialog box—you'll see the query that searches for entries created in the last seven days listed there.

The Phone Calls view lists all the entries with the entry type set as Phone Call. This is useful only if you remember to record all your phone calls in Outlook. A partial record of phone calls could be misleading and might paint the wrong picture if you are recording these for a time/payment-booking system.

Finally, the Outlook Data Files view lists all entries for the Journal based on the Outlook data file you are scrutinizing.

CHAPTER 7

Task Management

We all have things to do. We all need to keep track of those things too, lest we get caught up in a web of consequences.

Today more task management systems, strategies, and products exist than it's possible to count, and each of them has at least one follower who swears by its merits. Many people want to use Outlook to manage their tasks simply because of its convenience: if you're forced into using Outlook for email and calendaring, why not make it a one-stop shop for your to-do list as well?

Nothing in Outlook 2007 will shake the task management world to its core, but it does offer numerous improvements over previous versions of the product. In this chapter, we'll cover how tasks in Outlook 2007 are arranged, how to use the new To-Do Bar, how to categorize and manage tasks, how to include others in your tasks, how to connect external programs to Outlook tasks, and how to do much more.

Reviewing the History of the Task Structure

You may have heard from fellow Outlook users about the resistance they have to using the task management functionality in Outlook 97, 2000, XP, or 2003. And it's understandable why those users have had such a hard time with the structure of defining, administering, and then reviewing tasks. It was unintuitive and somewhat difficult to find where to enter a single task and then input the details surrounding it. And once you did stumble upon and successfully create a task list in Outlook, you were immediately frustrated by how difficult it was to integrate your view of your day between the calendar, Journal, task list, and email. The Tasks module in previous versions of Outlook felt like an afterthought.

However, during the process of redesigning Outlook 2007's Tasks module, Microsoft conducted extensive usability surveys and both fixed the problems with its current task module structure and determined what sort of time management strategies everyday workers were using. In this day of the *Taking Back Your Life* and *Getting Things Done* books and new time management strategies, some core pillars of wisdom have emerged, as follows:

- There is definitely a significant need for a to-do list. The naysayers who claim such task lists are outdated or inefficient aren't being practical or realistic.
- Most users need to track completion dates and deadlines for the items on their to-do lists, if only to know when to renegotiate the time they're given to complete an item.
- There is some value in breaking out to-do list items and categorizing them by the overall "project" under which they fall.
- There shouldn't be multiple task lists; one organized, consistent list is best.

In response to the criticisms and the standard advice dispensed by these time management specialists, the Office team radically redesigned the entire notion of tasks in Outlook 2007, including how they're displayed, integrated, and managed within the various areas of the user interface.

Entering Task Items

Outlook 2007 makes it much easier to enter tasks into the system. First, the Task Input panel is a simple way to enter a one-line description of the item you want to track. The idea is to get your to-do list out of your mind and into a trusted list. The Task Input panel is a quick way to do just that. Figure 7-1 shows this panel.

For a lot of us, tasks come in the form of emails—either messages from our superiors letting us know of tasks or from peers who include attachments that relate to the task. For example, we receive documents to review from colleagues many times a day, and each of those reviews needs to take place on a schedule. In Outlook 2003, we extensively used the follow-up flags, which were effective as an email to-do list; however, it was difficult to integrate deadline scheduling into that list. We ended up modifying the subject line of each email with the due date for the tasks outlined within the message. In Outlook 2007, however, associating a date with an email that needs follow-up is quite simple—you can simply right-click the flag placeholder beside each message and select the appropriate date to be reminded of the item. Useful "hotlinks" include Today, Tomorrow, and Next Week, and you can define your own date by selecting Custom. Figure 7-2 shows this menu.

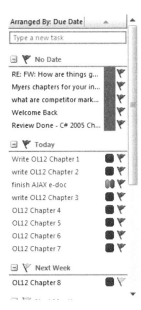

Figure 7-1. The Task Input panel

Figure 7-2. Date-based flagging in action

Using the To-Do Bar

In previous versions of Outlook, there was a "home page" of sorts known as Outlook Today that gave a limited, simplistic view of your upcoming appointments over the next few days, the number of unread email messages in a few folders, and a straight rundown of your task list and any associated deadlines you had inputted. Worst of all, you couldn't look at this quasi-integrated list and your email at the same time, and you couldn't see a graphical view of your calendar and task list from this integrated page (you could from the calendar page, but not from your inbox or any other folder).

The idea of making these contexts—in other words, the view in which you're currently using Outlook—both consistent and transparent was heavy on the minds of the Outlook 2007 designers. The result of this process was the To-Do Bar, a thoroughly integrated view of your calendar, upcoming appointments, tasks, and task-entry pad that remains tucked away when you don't need it but is available in any window in which you want to see it. Figure 7-3 shows the To-Do Bar.

Figure 7-3. The To-Do Bar

The To-Do Bar includes both the task list and any flagged email items you've created, as well as a list of your next two to three upcoming appointments, depending on the screen resolution you're currently using. The flags are even shaded—the brighter the flag, the closer you are to the due date of that particular task. Even better, the task list is integrated throughout other Office products. For example, you can flag individual notes with Microsoft OneNote, and such flags will automatically (and most important, seamlessly) display in the task list. You can also link lists of items to do that reside on SharePoint 2007 team sites to the task list if they're currently assigned to you, thus giving you a unified view of everything that requires your time and attention without having multiple lists spread through several different products and websites.

You may have an elaborate task structure that involves subfolders of tasks that are categorized; for example, under the main Tasks folder, you might have Personal, Business 1, Business 2, Gifts to Get, Letters to Write, and so on. By default, Outlook 2007 will put all tasks, no matter their location in your folder structure, on the To-Do Bar. But you may want to exclude tasks in certain folders from appearing on the bar to give you a cleaner look or to protect some sensitive task details from being displayed in every view. To do so, follow these steps:

1. Click the Arrange By header in the To-Do Bar, and select Custom.
2. In the Customize View dialog box, click the Filter button.
3. Click the Advanced tab.
4. Under Fields, select All Task Fields, and then select In Folder.
5. Click the Condition drop-down list, and select Doesn't Contain.
6. In the Value field, type the name of the folder you want to exclude, and then click Add to List. Figure 7-4 shows this step.

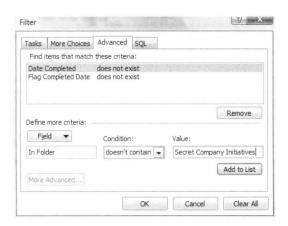

Figure 7-4. Filtering tasks on the To-Do Bar

Viewing Existing Tasks

If you're looking for a deeper view of your tasks than the To-Do Bar affords, then the Tasks view is for you. The Tasks module shows flagged email and contacts, along with all your Outlook tasks, SharePoint task lists to which you subscribe, task lists you define in Microsoft OneNote, and any tasks assigned to you through a corporate Microsoft Project Server machine. Figure 7-5 shows the default Tasks view.

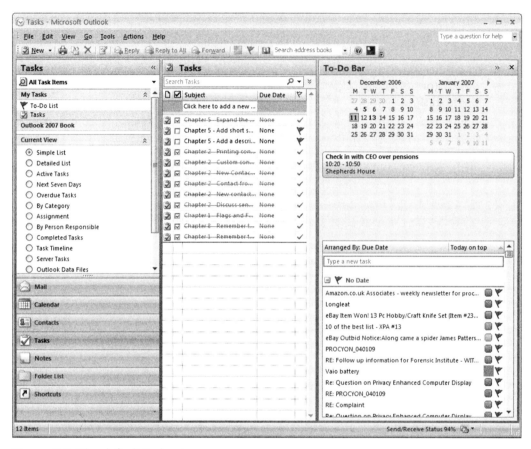

Figure 7-5. The default Tasks view

You'll notice that the Reading pane is on, much like in the Mail view, so you can scroll through your tasks and see all the details easily without having to open each one to get the pertinent information; you can also adjust the positioning of the Reading pane from the View ➤ Reading Pane menu.

The main advantage of viewing the Tasks module this way is the ability to sort and manage your tasks in different ways. By selecting different options from the filter list in the left pane, you can easily see just your active tasks, items to do over the next seven days, tasks that are beyond their deadline, tasks listed just from a Project Server connection, or completed tasks. Such views are useful for completing various kinds of status reports—for instance, what did you get done this week?

Also note the multiple task folders in the top left of this view. The To-Do Bar task list is a search folder (see Chapter 3 for more about search folders) that aggregates all flagged mail, contacts, and tasks from across your different mailbox and data stores and displays them in the To-Do Bar. You can edit the list directly from this view. Since search folders cannot be shared through Exchange, cannot be drop targets when items are dragged to them, and cannot have subfolders, Outlook includes a simple folder called Tasks that contains only the tasks in your current mailbox or data store (a .pst file or otherwise). The Tasks folder is a standard folder and supports all the different actions that the search folder doesn't support.

In the course of working with your tasks, you might find the need to assign a task to another employee of your organization. It's easy to do this from within the Tasks module (or the To-Do Bar, for that matter); simply double-click the task, and click the Assign Task button on the Ribbon. The task will transform into a hybrid email message, as shown in Figure 7-6. Just enter the user's name, and select whether to be kept up-to-date about when the task is completed and whether to keep a copy of the task on your own list for record-keeping purposes. If you want to be reminded of this task later, click the Follow Up button to remind you to contact the assignee about the status later.

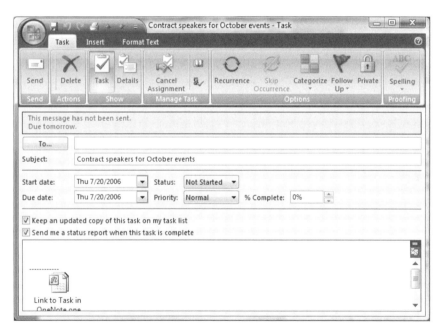

Figure 7-6. Assigning a task

Similarly, your supervisor may want to be kept up-to-date about the status of your tasks, particularly those she directly assigns you via Outlook. You can send the status, along with your own personal notes, to her by opening the task and clicking the Send Status Report button. Again, a hybrid email window will open, and the current status of the task will be pasted into the body of the task (as shown in Figure 7-7). Enter an addressee, add some notes if you want, click to be reminded to follow up if you need it, and then click Send.

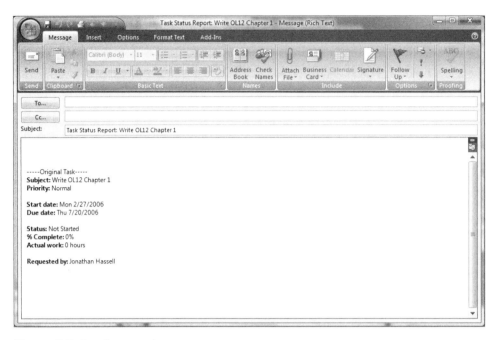

Figure 7-7. Sending a task status report

Finally, if you simply want another user to be able to see your task list, and not necessarily send status reports on every task to her directly, that's a simple process. Enter the Tasks module, and from the left pane, click the Share My Tasks folder link. Enter the username of the person you want to share with, add a personal note if you want, click the checkbox if you need reciprocal access to the recipient's task list, and then click Send.

Scheduling for Tasks on the Calendar

Another tenet of time management is actually setting aside defined blocks of time during your day to complete the items appearing on your to-do list. It's all too easy to schedule meetings all day long only to realize that when you return to your office after seven straight hours in a conference room that you have two proposals to review, updated spreadsheets to send to your sales team, and a presentation to finish before tomorrow. Blocking out time on your schedule to complete certain tasks will help you avoid such an unpleasant situation whenever possible.

In Outlook 2007, it became much easier to do just that—the Calendar view now shows your task list broken out in relevant blocks. In the Week view, which is the default and is limited to the typical work week (Monday through Friday), you see the tasks on your list that have been assigned to that particular day, as shown in Figure 7-8.

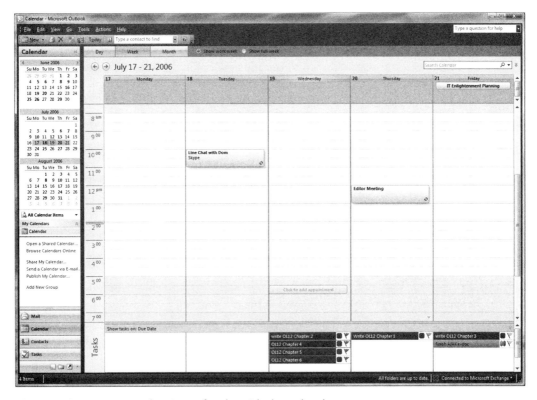

Figure 7-8. Integrating the view of tasks with the calendar

| **NOTE** The task list, as shown in Figure 7-8, also appears when you view the calendar in Day view.

To schedule a task, you can simply drag it from the task list to the appropriate time block on the calendar, and Outlook will automatically schedule 30 minutes in which to complete the task. You can drag the boundaries of the task after the first step if you need more time. Of course, this process preserves all the detail information contained within the original task or flagged email item. And you can review on your progress throughout the week to see what you accomplished and what inevitably didn't get done. (The task list automatically advances overdue but incomplete tasks to the current day; you don't need to do this manually.)

Categorizing and Searching for Your Tasks

As you know from Chapter 9, you can assign a category to every common Outlook object, including task items, and then color-code them. The idea here is that you can categorize your tasks by project, assigning green, for example, to all mail, calendar items, tasks, and notes that relate to the same overall set of objectives. (Refer to Chapter 9 to learn how to use categories.)

Perhaps the most useful way to use the new colored categories is finding categorized mailbox items using the instant search feature within Outlook. The instant search box appears at the top of the middle pane in the Mail view; just click the chevron to expose more options. You can enter any keywords you like, but to filter search results on just certain categories, click the Add Criteria button, select Categories to add the option to the list, and then click the drop-down list to select the appropriate category. You can see this process in Figure 7-9.

Figure 7-9. Searching for categorized items

Connecting SharePoint Task Lists to Outlook

Many corporations are using SharePoint technologies to facilitate team collaboration and document storage. However, Outlook has previously had minimal integration with SharePoint, particularly with respect to tasks: users had to either manually keep track of which tasks were assigned to them on the SharePoint site and update their copy of Outlook with the appropriate information; or worse, they simply ignored the SharePoint task list and figured they would be nudged anytime information was needed from them. This was clearly not the best situation.

In Outlook 2007, you can connect SharePoint task lists to Outlook and have their data integrated both into the main Tasks module and in the To-Do Bar views so you have one-stop shopping for monitoring your tasks. You do need Windows Share-Point Services 3.0 and Outlook 2007—previous versions of either product don't have the capability to connect to each other.

You initiate the connection from the SharePoint side. First, navigate to the list you want to connect, and then from the Actions menu, select Connect to Outlook. You may have to acknowledge a Windows Firewall warning that Outlook wants to retrieve data externally.

Next, Outlook will open a dialog box, shown in Figure 7-10, asking you to accept the new task list and giving you the option to configure it.

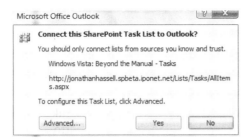

Figure 7-10. Accepting a SharePoint task list

Clicking Advanced opens the SharePoint List Options dialog box (shown in Figure 7-11), which allows you to change the name of the task list's folder as it will appear within Outlook, add a description of the task list for further reference, keep the task list only on the machine you're currently using, and confirm you want to poll the SharePoint site for updates as often as your administrator recommends. Click OK when you're done, and then the task list will integrate itself with Outlook in a few seconds.

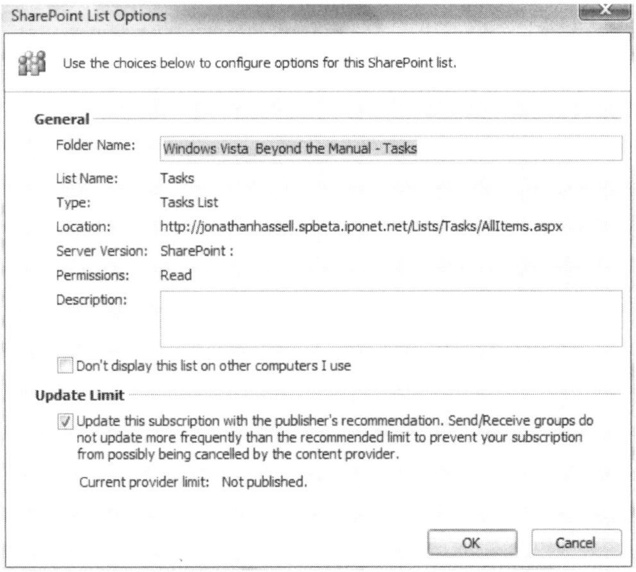

Figure 7-11. Configuring advanced SharePoint task list options within Outlook

Any tasks that were specifically assigned to you will show up in the To-Do Bar automatically, sorted according to your current grouping. If you want to see only the tasks on the SharePoint site, you can go to the Tasks module and, in the top-left corner, click the SharePoint task list's name. The information will synchronize with the SharePoint site automatically and display the most updated information possible.

There are some interesting differences between a regular task that resides only within Outlook and one that is part of a connected SharePoint list, as follows:

- Assigning and reassigning tasks is quite straightforward. Although regular Outlook tasks have an Assigned To field that can be populated, on a task that is part of a SharePoint list, the contents of the Assigned To field are set up to the SharePoint site and made public, so the entire team can look to determine which members are doing which tasks.

- Anyone can reassign a SharePoint task to anyone else. A regular Outlook task, by virtue of Outlook being a personal client installed on someone's machine, can be reassigned only by that user. SharePoint-based tasks, however, can be passed around without restriction.

- The body of SharePoint tasks is free-form and can accept any style of input. As tasks are passed around, each team member who is at some point an assignee can make a comment in the body of the task, documenting his actions, potential pitfalls, or questions that still remain. Two benefits emerge: a complete history of the actions a task undergoes is maintained if people write in the body of the task, and this history is public. It doesn't just sit in someone's inbox; it's available to any member of the SharePoint site with the appropriate credentials.

- Finally, SharePoint tasks document the last team member to touch them. In the bottom-right corner of the task's detail view, you can see who last updated an item and the time that update took place, as shown in Figure 7-12.

Figure 7-12. Viewing last-modification information on a SharePoint task

Synchronizing OneNote Tasks with Outlook

Microsoft OneNote is a note-taking program that was designed particularly for use with Tablet PCs—machines that allow you to write on the screen with a pen-like stylus. OneNote allows you to write free-form, as if you were scratching notes on a legal pad, and then converts your handwriting to text by virtue of a reasonably good optical character recognition system. You don't have to use a Tablet PC with OneNote; you can simply use a keyboard and type directly into the program. Regardless of how you use OneNote, the program is ideal for taking notes in meetings. And from many meetings arise action points.

With Outlook 2007, you can flag certain lines in a OneNote document as items to follow up on. They will automatically be converted to tasks in Outlook and populate the Tasks module and your To-Do Bar based on the flag you select in OneNote. For example, Figure 7-13 shows some meeting notes and actions that have been jotted down in OneNote. To synchronize them with Outlook, highlight them, and select a date from the Follow Up menu.

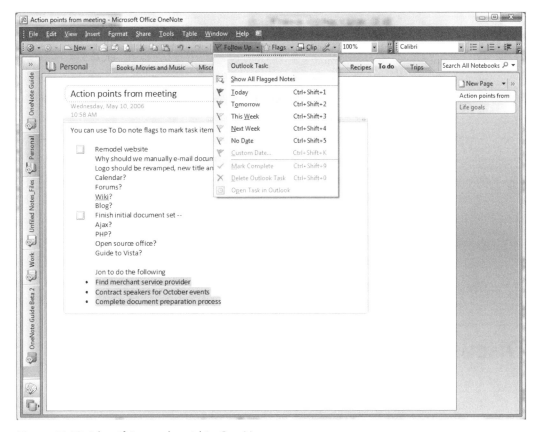

Figure 7-13. Identifying tasks within OneNote

In this example, let's assume the user needs to get these items completed as soon as he can but the meeting took place at the end of the workday, so select Tomorrow from the menu. The tasks will automatically shift to Outlook in the background, and OneNote will display the follow-up flag icon beside each of the bullet points to show that the item is synchronized.

Within Outlook, the item shows up in all the proper places. To edit the task further, find the task in Outlook, and double-click it; alternatively, right-click the item from within OneNote, and select Open Task in Outlook. The task window will open. You will also see a link to the item in OneNote within the body of the task in the

Outlook window, as shown in Figure 7-14. This is useful to place the task within the proper context of the meeting if your memory is hazy as to exactly why you need to do the task.

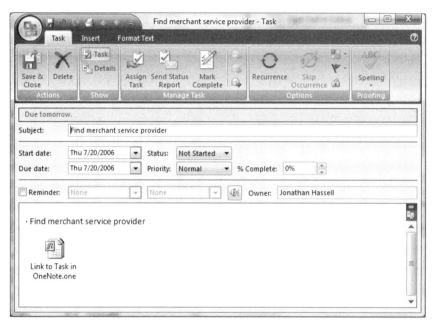

Figure 7-14. Identifying tasks within OneNote

Discussing Subtasks

In the past, a moderately small but vociferous group of Outlook users have demanded the ability in future versions of the product to create hierarchies of tasks, with dependencies and relationships between all the tasks. It seems that for a lot of people, a tree-like structure is the best way to organize their thoughts and to-do lists—sort of like a crude mind map. Outlook has never supported this, and at least in this version, it continues that streak, disappointing many existing users and scaring off others.

Apparently, the inside story goes something like this: in usability studies conducted before the development of the Office 2007 suite began, researchers found that less than 2 percent of Outlook customers even used tasks at all. These analysts supposed that this dismal figure was because configuring, managing, and using tasks in Outlook was too complicated. Tasks were masked in a separate area of the product that wasn't well integrated throughout the rest of the program, and they weren't easy to use with the calendar; in general, they were simply too obstinate to rely on. Thus, in the product team's opinion, it was better to spend development effort for Outlook 2007 on making tasks easier to use throughout the various views of the product than it was to make an effort to satisfy the growing demand for subtasks—after all, if tasks are too hard to use already, then adding a hierarchy would simply muddy the waters even more, right? However, some other rumors emerged, the most common one being that Microsoft didn't want to cannibalize sales of Microsoft Project by adding more than the simplest of task management capabilities to Outlook. Whatever the reason, subtasks are not an included feature.

What you can do about this situation, however, is work around the absence of subtasks by using some of the newer capabilities of Outlook. Here are some alternatives, any of which can work by itself or in combination with the other alternatives:

Use a dedicated category as a master task, and use tasks as individual "subtasks": This is especially effective if you sort the To-Do Bar by category, giving you effectively a hierarchical view of your "subtasks" by a main task.

Embed subtasks with a single task: Outlook 2007 allows you to edit the body of tasks using rich-text features from Word 2007, so you can make a bulleted list of subtasks within an individual Outlook task and use strikethrough or delete the appropriate bullet points as you complete tasks.

Make categories act as both main tasks and next-action identifiers: Since you can apply multiple categories to the same item, you could apply both an identifying project category to a task and the appropriate next-action category to the item. For instance, a task called "Buy book" could be labeled under the Product Research category but also the Errands category so you would remember the buy the book the next time you're shopping.

Using Tasks Effectively

Here are some suggestions on how to get the most out of Outlook tasks, quickly and efficiently:

Drag and drop tasks in a list view to change their order: If you like to plan your day completely in the morning and follow your to-do list in an exact order, then simply drag and reorder tasks in the To-Do Bar or in the general Tasks view to whatever order you want. Outlook will remember the order across views and present it consistently throughout the product.

Refresh yourself the context of a mail-based task by reading the entire thread: If you've created a task based on a mail message, flagged it for follow-up two weeks later, and now you have no idea what went on in the associated thread because it's fourteen days later, just click the InfoBar in the right pane, and from the pop-up menu, select Find Related Messages. You'll then get all the messages in that thread in a dialog box. To make it even easier, in the resulting dialog box click the Arranged By bar, and select Conversation to read all the related messages in threaded fashion.

Instruct Outlook to automatically create reminders for all the mail you flag: It's easy to automatically give yourself a nudge on mail-based tasks you flag. In Outlook 2007, select Tool ➤ Options, click the Task Options button, and then check the box entitled Set Reminders on Tasks with Due Dates. (By default, in Outlook 2007, it's not checked.)

Remember the keyboard shortcut to create a task from any area of Outlook 2007: Pressing Ctrl+Shift+K will open a new task window, ready and waiting for your information.

Associate a shortcut key with a commonly assigned color category: Right-click any item, select Categories ➤ All Categories, and then click a category for which you want a shortcut key. Then, select a Ctrl+<function key> combination from the drop-down list on the right side of the window. Your selection automatically updates in the window.

Grab tasks and action items from other information stores, and have them appear on your To-Do Bar: Make sure you go to the Folder List view in the Navigation pane, and then right-click each of the stores for which you want to see in action, and select Properties for [Store Name]. On the General tab, check the Display Reminders and Tasks from this Folder box in the To-Do Bar. Click Apply, click OK, and then restart Outlook 2007 for this change to fully take effect.

Customize table-style views to show the information you really need: You can change the sort of, say, your completed tasks to alphabetize them by their subject line to make it easier to find a specific task. Take it one step further, and add a field for the percentage complete by right-clicking the header of any table and selecting Field Chooser. Just drag the desired property out of the box and onto the table. To get rid of a field from the view, click and drag it out of the view. You can also group table-style views by a certain field by right-clicking the field header and selecting Group by This Field, which useful for grabbing all the tasks due on Monday, for example.

CHAPTER 8

Storage Management

You will have noticed by now that when you view email in Outlook, if that email is spread across multiple folders, these folders look very much like those you'd see in Windows Explorer when viewing the file system (see Figure 8-1).

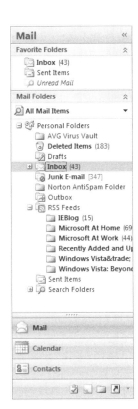

Figure 8-1. In the user interface, Outlook folders appear much like file system folders.

Nevertheless, the folders in Outlook are nothing like folders in the file system; instead, they're stored in a single location in a database, with the view in Outlook derived from metadata associated with each item in the data store.

Outlook provides this kind of data storage in a variety of ways, and it's important to understand the differences between each of these methods in order to best select what's good for you.

The three storage methods we'll discuss in this chapter are as follows:

- Storing data in a personal folder (PST)
- Storing data in an offline folder (OST)
- Storing data on a Microsoft Exchange Server machine

In Outlook terms, a *data store* is a database that contains all your email, your contacts, any notes you've taken, any tasks you've created, your calendar appointments, and your account information. These data stores can either be local to your PC if you are operating in a stand-alone environment (the PST and OST files) or be on a server if you happen to be running Outlook in a Windows domain that is connected to an Exchange Server computer.

Users are allocated a default data store when their Outlook profile is first created; for example, a user's profile might have been assigned on an Exchange Server computer for corporate email. However, you can assign extra data stores to a user's profile to allow for the partition of data between individual containers in order to achieve a level of separation for security purposes between personal and business email. You may also consider assigning a second data store to be used to back up the default data store in the event the default data store becomes corrupt.

Introducing Personal Folders

You can use a personal folder file (PST) to store your contacts, calendar entries, email messages, and tasks. You can have as many PST files as needed, all simultaneously attached to your Outlook profile. Each of these PST files will be presented as a separate folder in the user interface.

The default PST file associated with your Outlook profile is called Outlook.pst and is stored in your user profile under the directory path of \Local Settings\ Application Data\Microsoft\Outlook\Outlook.pst.

To see a list of the data stores installed on your system, right-click the Outlook icon on the Start menu (or on your desktop), select Properties from the context menu, and then click Data Files (see Figure 8-2).

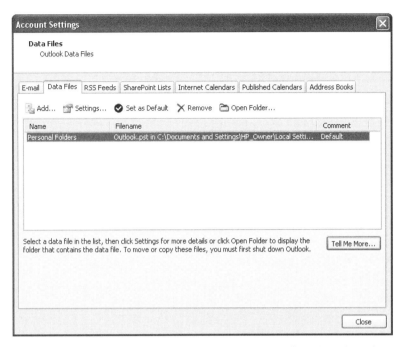

Figure 8-2. All data stores that Outlook is aware of are listed on the Data Files tab.

> **NOTE** You can add security to a PST file by password-protecting it. That way, you can use a PST file for archiving old email, and then you can store it somewhere safe. In the event of a problem occurring with your primary system and Outlook being reinstalled, you can reattach your old PST file to your new system, enter the password, and start using your old email again.

In this dialog box, you can add a new data file, change the settings of an existing data file (such as the security settings), change which data file is the default, remove a data file, and open the folder the PST files are stored in using Windows Explorer.

To look at the details of a specific data store, you can highlight the store in question, and click Settings; alternatively, you can simply double-click it. The opens the Personal Folders dialog box, as shown in Figure 8-3.

Figure 8-3. Change the settings of an existing PST file.

Adding New PST Files

Adding extra PST data stores to Outlook is easy. You do this using the Outlook icon on the Start menu (or the desktop icon if you've chosen to clutter your desktop).

To add the new data store, perform the following procedure:

1. Right-click the Outlook icon on the Start menu, and then select Properties.
2. When you see the Mail Setup dialog box, click the Data Files button.
3. Click the Add button on the toolbar to open the New Outlook Data File dialog box, as shown in Figure 8-4.

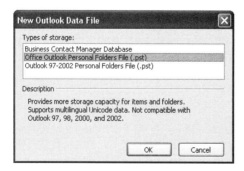

Figure 8-4. Select the appropriate data store type from the list.

NOTE If you are intending to use this data store to import information from an older version of Outlook (from Outlook 97 through Outlook 2002), then you should select the Outlook 97–2002 Personal Folders File (.pst) option from the list. It's important to realize from Outlook 2003 onward, the format of the .pst file has changed; in addition, the later version of .pst files are not compatible with earlier versions of Outlook.

4. Select Office Outlook Personal Folders File (.pst) from the list, and then click OK.

5. In the Create or Open Outlook Data File dialog box, shown in Figure 8-5, give the new data store file a meaningful name, and then click OK.

NOTE The default storage location for .pst files is \Local Settings\ Application Data\Microsoft\Outlook\Outlook.pst. If you do not want to store your new data file in this location, you can click Browse Folders to instruct Outlook where this new file should be located. Clicking the Tools drop-down menu allows you to map a network drive to locate the new file on a remote system.

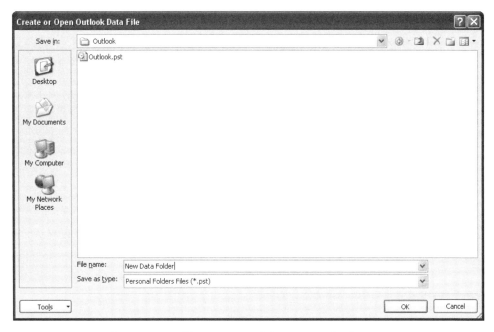

Figure 8-5. Give the new .pst file a meaningful name, and select an appropriate location.

6. Next, you'll see the Create Microsoft Personal Folders dialog box, as shown in Figure 8-6. If you want to password-protect this .pst file, you can do so at this stage. You should also type the name you want to see listed in Outlook's user interface to identify the new data store—this can be different from the physical filename you entered during the previous step. When you're ready to create the data store, click OK.

Figure 8-6. Assign a password to the .pst file to protect its contents from unauthorized access.

NOTE You have the option of storing your password in the local password list. This will store your new data store password in the local system's password cache, removing the need for you to repeatedly type it each time you attempt to access the file. If you do not save the password locally, your data is certainly more secure; however, you will have to retype the password each time you try to access it.

Once the data store is created, you'll see it appear in the list of personal folders available on the Data Files tab in the Account Settings dialog box, as shown in Figure 8-7.

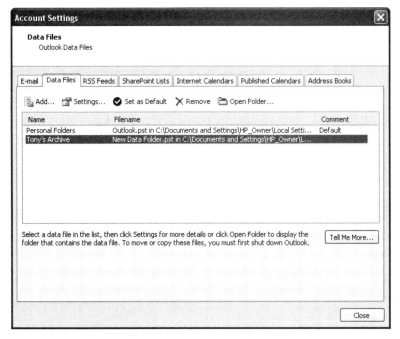

Figure 8-7. New data files are added to the list in the primary Account Settings dialog box.

Removing PST Files

You can easily remove a data store that is no longer required by going through the Account Settings dialog box.

The process for removing an unwanted .pst file is as follows:

1. Right-click the Outlook icon on the Start menu, and then select Properties.

2. When you see the Mail Setup dialog box, click the Data Files button.

3. Highlight the personal folder file you want to delete, and then click Remove.

4. Confirm you want to proceed by clicking Yes.

This removes the folder from Outlook but not from the file system. This way, you can later return to the .pst file and add it again.

Attaching an Existing PST File

Attaching an existing .pst file to Outlook is straightforward. You do this using the Add function in the Account Settings dialog box, much in the same way you would add a new personal folder. The difference this time is that you need to locate the existing .pst file on the file system and use it instead.

Outlook will prompt you for a password if the .pst file is protected (see Figure 8-8), and again, as before, you have the option to store the password in the local password list if you deem this necessary.

Figure 8-8. You will need the password of an existing .pst file before you can add it into Outlook.

Introducing Offline Folders

If you are using Outlook as a client to an Exchange Server computer, your data will be stored on the server as usual, with nothing held locally. However, sometimes this is not always the best configuration for users; for example, when a mobile worker is not always in direct network contact with the Exchange Server computer, she still needs to access items in her mailbox, calendar, and Journal offline.

The concept of offline storage allows you to essentially carry on working in Outlook even though you are not connected to your primary Exchange Server system.

Two options are available for users wanting to work offline:

- Offline storage files (OST files)
- Cached Exchange Mode

The difference between the two methods is subtle but worth understanding nonetheless.

OST Files

An OST file stores a local copy of your Exchange data store and is active when you have no connection to the Exchange Server. In this instance, you will work locally in the OST file.

The OST file stores email messages, contacts, calendar entries, and tasks in the same way as a PST file, with the only difference that Outlook must manage the synchronization between the OST file and Exchange Server when a network connection is established.

When you are connected to the network, you will always use the Exchange Server mailbox, with synchronization occurring from the server to the client. When you are not connected to the Exchange Server and are operating offline, you will work exclusively in the OST file, and the synchronization on reconnection to the server will flow from the client to the server for changes made in the OST file and from the server to the client for new items not yet sent to the user.

> **NOTE** Synchronization should always ensure that the latest data item is nominated as authoritative. In this way, if you delete items in your OST file while working offline, those items will be deleted in Exchange Server when you reconnect. Similarly, new items in Exchange Server will be replicated to the OST file on reconnection, such as new calendar items and email messages.

Cached Exchange Mode

Cached Exchange Mode works slightly differently than standard offline folders in that the local OST file being used to cache Exchange Server (and it's still the same OST technology under the hood) is used exclusively, irrespective of whether you are connected to the Exchange Server. In this way, synchronization is easier, and you are always positive you are working on the latest information.

When you synchronize with Exchange Server, all the work you have done in your OST file is replicated to Exchange Server, and all the new messages are transmitted to the cache.

We cover Cached Exchange Mode in more detail in Chapter 12.

Using OST Files

When you add an Exchange Server account to your Outlook profile, Cached Exchange Mode is initiated by default. You can decide at this stage to not use Cached Exchange Mode and instead turn it on later if desired.

To switch offline storage for an Exchange account where it is not initially activated, do the following:

1. Right-click the Outlook icon on the Start menu, and then select Properties.
2. When you see the Mail Setup dialog box, click the E-mail Accounts button.
3. Highlight the Exchange Server account, and then click Change.
4. Click More Settings, and then click the Advanced tab in the dialog box.
5. Click Offline Folder File Settings.
6. Select a file and path name and the encryption requirements of the OST file, and then click OK.
7. Back in the Account Settings dialog box, click Next, and then click Finish.

If you want to subsequently switch on Cached Exchange Mode, you'll need to go through the process outlined here, but you should select the Use Cached Exchange Mode checkbox before you click Finish.

Exploring the Message Delivery Options

The default data store will be used for the delivery of all messages unless you specify otherwise. If you look at the list of data stores available on your system (right-click the Outlook icon on the Start menu, and then select Properties ➤ Data Files), you'll see the Default marker on the Comment column next to your default store.

You can link ancillary data stores to individual email accounts and use them as the target for each account if desired. In this way, you can split up email from different sources into different data stores and protect each one in whatever way that's applicable to you.

To use a new data store and attach it to a specific email account, you should switch to the E-mail tab in the Account Settings dialog box and highlight the account you want to change to the new data store, as shown in Figure 8-9.

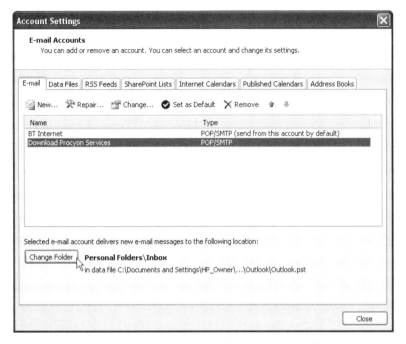

Figure 8-9. Configure Outlook to send emails from different accounts to separate PST files.

Next, click the Change Folder button, highlight the PST folder, and then click New Folder. Type the name of the new folder to be used within the data store for delivery of the email account items, as shown in Figure 8-10.

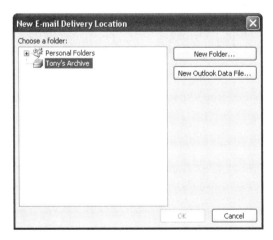

Figure 8-10. Add a new folder to a data file to act as the target for an email account.

When you're done, click OK to return to the Account Settings dialog box. Notice that the new folder location appears at the bottom of the screen. On returning to the Outlook user interface, the new data store will appear on the left side of the screen, and you'll see the new folder is contained within it. All email subsequently received by that email account will be directed into the new folder within the new PST data store.

Backing Up and Restoring Personal Folders

When you use Outlook connected to an Exchange Server, you don't have to worry so much about loss of data—unless you have little trust in your system's administrator, that is. However, if you are using personal folders (PST) for storing data from an Internet account (or for archiving data from an Exchange Server account), you will need to be familiar with the methods available for backing up and restoring this data in the event of a system crash.

Now, the bad news is that no special backup capability is built into Outlook; instead, you are required to back up the PST files yourself, either by taking a straightforward file copy of the files from the file system or by using a separate backup system, such as Windows Backup.

By far the better of the two options is to integrate your PST backup requirements into a system-wide backup regime, whereby you are protecting not only your Outlook data but the rest of your PC data as well. The system backup facility available with Windows 2000, Windows XP, and Windows Vista will allow you to specify the path to where your PST files are located and ensure that any backup schedule you create includes a regular copy of your Outlook folders, as shown in Figure 8-11.

If you do not have a backup solution in place and are still concerned about your personal folder data, make a copy of the PST files from the file system and store them safely on a writable CD or a removable hard drive, preferably offsite.

Restoring your PST files is as easy as it was to add a new file. You need to locate the backup (either using the backup software or providing the writable media) and extract the relevant PST file. It's then a simple matter of following the instructions for adding an existing PST file (covered earlier in this chapter), providing the password where necessary.

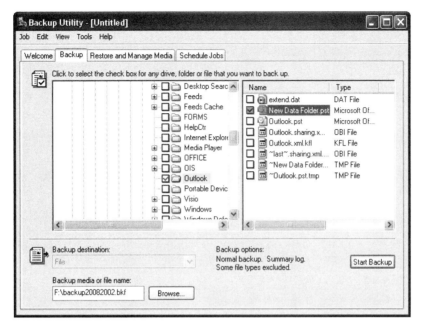

Figure 8-11. Use your PC's backup solution to back up and restore your Outlook personal folder.

Remember, if you are recovering a PST file from a remote location into an existing, operating version of Outlook, you'll need to either change the email account to store data in the new location (if this is what you desire) or change the new folder to be the default data store.

CHAPTER 9

Color Categories

I n Outlook terms, a *category* is a keyword or phrase used to assist you in organizing and monitoring Outlook objects, such as emails, contacts, appointments, tasks, and notes. These Outlook objects are known simply as *items*, and we will refer to them henceforth as such.

The main power of using categories in Outlook comes from the inherent object-oriented nature of their ability to group items under a specific topic, such as those related to a work task or a private appointment; then you can use the category to search, sort, and filter data relevant to that topic.

> **NOTE** Categories are metadata you apply to Outlook objects in much the same way you apply metadata to multimedia files in your Music folder. For example, you can group items into collections that have practical meanings, rather than the more traditional contiguous fashion where items appear in standard containers such as your inbox.

Categories have evolved significantly from Outlook 2003 and are now displayed as vibrant color-coded stamps that you can apply to practically every item that exists within your Outlook information store.

You can use categories in as flexible a way as you like and to whatever extent you think appropriate, allowing you to adjust the way you both store and view information and allowing you to work in whatever way suits you best. To this end, you can create a logical folder structure of objects that are fixed and then use categories to extract information across the entire set of folders into a task-oriented view. For example, if you created a category dedicated to work on a project called Real Estate, you could extract information from your Calendar, Mail, Tasks, Contacts, and Notes folders all marked with the Real Estate category. If Real Estate were color-coded blue, everything related to the project would stand out at a moment's notice with a bright blue flash next to it.

Using the Color Categories List

When you first start using Outlook, the categories available have generic names with color codes of blue, green, orange, purple, red, and yellow, as shown in Figure 9-1.

It's advisable that you begin by determining which categories you will need in your day-to-day activities and then redefine the default ones with meaningful names. Sticking to your preferences (and believe us, once you are disciplined in using categories, you'll never look back), for example, you could rename Red Category to Urgent, and you will treat any items flashed with red immediately with the appropriate level of attention.

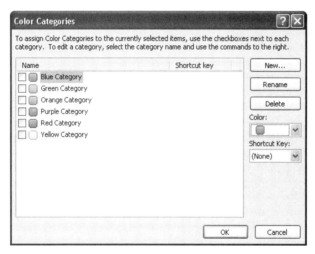

Figure 9-1. Outlook comes with six default categories of generic names.

In previous versions of Outlook, you did this using the Master Category list, which was once quite complicated to operate. No longer, however, is this the case. You now use the Color Categories list, and color categories are simple to use yet highly effective in presenting groupings of like items in a way never before achieved in Outlook.

You can access the Color Categories list by selecting Edit ➤ Categorize ➤ All Categories.

You can easily create new categories to add to your Color Categories list as new items arrive in your inbox or appointments arrive in your calendar. Alternatively, you can set up a list of categories in the Color Categories list in advance and assign items to the categories as the items arrive.

The system is extremely flexible and allows you to create and remove categories as you work, which means you can quickly react to a situation and set up a new functional area of interest on the fly.

Also, you can assign items to multiple categories, meaning you can be as creative as you want when labeling your life in Outlook as you require. For example, you could have one category dedicated to an item's source (such as your boss) and another related to the project you're working on (such as Real Estate).

> **TIP** Users of Microsoft Schedule+ will be pleased to know they can assign categories automatically as tasks are imported into Outlook.

Categories defined in the Color Categories list are pervasive across all object types in Outlook, applying equally to mail, appointments, contacts, tasks, and notes.

Adding, Modifying, and Using Categories

When you first decide to start using categories, you should consider renaming the ones you use since the default names are somewhat meaningless.

You have two options:

- Rename each category as you use it, deciding upon its purpose when you first assign it.
- Rename all necessary categories in advance.

Taking email as an example, highlight an email you would like to assign a category to, right-click the item in the inbox, and then select Categorize from the context menu. You'll immediately see another context menu spring out to the side, displaying your six default categories from Blue Category to Yellow Category. However, we'll first show how to rename an existing category. Outlook is clever enough to realize you haven't worked with this category before, so it offers you a dialog box (shown in Figure 9-2) to change its name. Changing the name at this stage will alter its name in the Color Categories list.

Figure 9-2. Change the default name to something more meaningful.

You can assign a keyboard shortcut (in the format of Ctrl+<function key>) to a category by selecting the appropriate Ctrl+<function key> sequence from the Shortcut Key drop-down list.

You can also modify the color identifier of a category by choosing from one of the 25 available color flashes in the Color drop-down list.

Adding and Modifying Categories

You can easily add new categories or modify existing ones to reflect a new working context through the Color Categories dialog box.

To get started, highlight any item (an email, task, or appointment), and then select Edit ➤ Categorize ➤ All Categories.

In the dialog box, as shown in Figure 9-3, you'll immediately see the list of already defined categories in your Color Categories list.

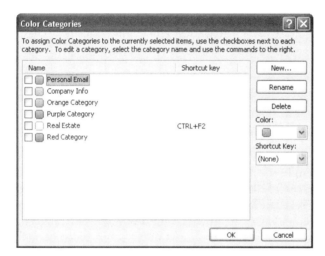

Figure 9-3. Categories are listed next to their color indicator field and keyboard shortcut.

On the right side of the dialog box you'll see three buttons: New, Rename, and Delete.

If you want to delete an existing category, highlight that category in the dialog box, and then click Delete. Confirm your intention by clicking OK when you see the warning.

> **NOTE** When you delete a category, you do not have to remove categorizations from items that have already been marked. That way, you can preserve categories for later searching and filtering even though they are deleted from the current list.

To change the name of a category, highlight the target category name, click Rename, and then type the new name in the textbox. Click OK when you're done.

Creating a new category is easy too. Click New, type the category name in the textbox, assign a color and a shortcut key, and then click OK (as shown in Figure 9-4).

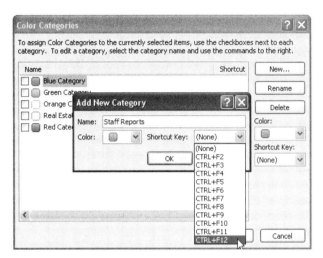

Figure 9-4. Adding new categories to the Color Categories list is easy.

Finally, in the Color Categories list, notice that each category has a checkbox to the left of the color designator. If you want to assign multiple categories to a collection of items at once, highlight the items in the background (holding down the Ctrl key and then right-clicking the items), and then select Edit ➤ Categorize ➤ All Categories. Now, check each category that allies to the items, and click OK.

Removing Category Assignments

You can quickly remove categories that have been assigned to items by right-clicking selected items, selecting Categorize from the context menu, and then selecting Clear All Categories. You can select multiple items by pressing the Ctrl key and then right-clicking any one of them; then follow the same procedure. This will remove all category assignments from all the items you have selected.

If you want to remove individual category assignments from an item yet you want to retain some that are still required, highlight the items, click Edit ➤ Categorize ➤ All Categories, and then uncheck the categories no longer required, as shown in Figure 9-5. Click OK when you are ready.

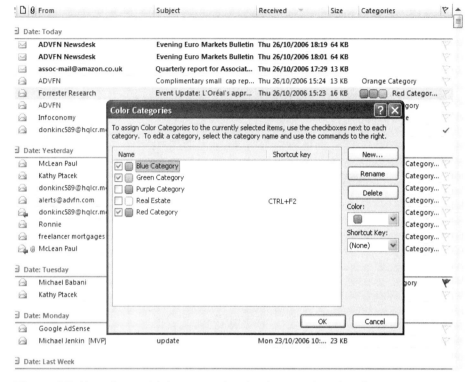

Figure 9-5. Unassign multiple categories simultaneously using the Color Categories list.

Assigning Quick Click

You can use what's known as the Quick Click option to automatically assign a category of your choice to any item when you click in the space under the Categories column for each email item in your inbox.

To set the category you want selected as your Quick Click category, select Edit ➤ Categorize ➤ Set Quick Click. This opens the dialog box shown in Figure 9-6.

Figure 9-6. Set the Quick Click option to your most commonly used category.

Select the category you want assigned to Quick Click from the drop-down list. This is most commonly used for categories that are either frequently assigned or alternatively for categories that carry a weighty significance, such as warnings or high-priority messages.

Using Category Search Folders

You can create a special search folder based on a category or collection of categories by selecting Edit ➤ Categorize ➤ Create Category Search Folder.

In the Customize Search Folder selection box at the bottom of the dialog box shown in Figure 9-7, you'll see that the default category is set to Any Category.

Figure 9-7. Search folders are highly configurable.

Click the Choose button, and then select (from the Color Categories list) the categories you want to construct your search around, remembering you can assign multiple categories by checking every checkbox that applies to your search. Next, ensure you are searching in the most appropriate mail folder (selecting the folder using the Search Mail In drop-down box), and then click OK.

The new search folder will appear in the folder view on the left side of the screen at the bottom beneath the Search Folders node.

CHAPTER 10

Customization

Once you start getting more familiar with Outlook 2007, using the plethora of functionality and features within this most capable product, you'll undoubtedly find that some aspects of the interface don't quite work for you in the way you'd like. You'll probably also find certain automation tasks that are not available with Outlook straight out of the box. Nevertheless, Outlook, like all its counterparts in the Office 2007 suite, is highly extensible, so you can customize it to your heart's content.

Often when we hear the term *customize*, especially in software, we immediately jump to the conclusion that this means *difficult*. It's easy to jump to the conclusion that customization means writing code, but, although possible, this is not necessary for the vast majority of customization tasks you might want to perform.

This chapter looks deep into the customization features available to Outlook users without ever having to look at Visual Basic for Applications (VBA); we'll leave a brief introduction into the world of VBA for Chapter 13.

Using Command-Line Switches to Start Outlook

Aside from using the regular method of starting Outlook (Start ➤ E-mail), you can also start Outlook by running the command outlook.exe. As with many commands, Outlook has several switches that control how it operates; you can apply these switches when you call the .exe file.

You can apply command-line switches to the outlook.exe file as part of a new shortcut you use when you start it, or you can call outlook.exe from the Run window (Windows logo+R).

You append a switch to the end of the filename using a forward slash followed by the appropriate switch, such as `outlook.exe /recycle`. Table 10-1 (a little later in this section) lists all the available switches.

> **NOTE** The Run command is available in both Windows XP and Windows Vista, although it's a little better hidden in Windows Vista on the Start menu. Both operating systems still support the Windows logo+R key sequence to open the dialog box, but to locate the Run command in the Start menu on Windows Vista, you'll need to delve into All Programs ➤ Accessories. When you use the Run window to start Outlook, you need to use the entire path prefix for the file (or alternatively use the Browse button in the Run window). Your command will look something like this: `"c:\program files\microsoft office\office12\outlook.exe" /recycle`. You need to ensure you include a blank space before the first switch (between `outlook.exe` and the `/`) and between each additional switch, and you also need to surround the path and filename with quotation marks.

To make an alternative way of starting Outlook more permanent, you should consider creating a desktop shortcut. This shortcut either can be called by clicking it when you log in or can be called automatically when you log in.

To create a shortcut for starting Outlook, do the following:

1. Right-click the desktop, and select New ➤ Shortcut.
2. In the Create Shortcut Wizard, type the Outlook command line you want to use to start Outlook, such as `"c:\program files\microsoft office\office12\outlook.exe" /recycle`. Click Next.
3. Type a meaningful name for this shortcut in the Type a Name for This Shortcut text box, and then click Finish.

When the wizard completes, the new shortcut will appear, ready for use, on your desktop.

> **NOTE** Windows Vista users can easily add the shortcut to the Start menu; just right-click the shortcut on the desktop, and then select Pin to Start Menu.

Table 10-1 shows all the switches available for starting Outlook.

Table 10-1. Outlook Start-up Switches

Switch	Description of Functionality
/a "<filename>"	Outlook creates a new email message with <filename> as an attachment.
/altvba "<vbafilename>"	Use this switch to open an alternative VBA program, rather than Outlook's default %appdata%\microsoft\outlook\vbaproject.otm.
/c messageclass	This creates a new item of the specified message class, based on Outlook forms or any other MAPI type; for example, ipm.activity creates an Outlook Journal entry, and ipm.stickynote creates an Outlook note.
/checkclient	This prompts the user to confirm the default manager of email messages, news, and contacts.
/cleancategories	This deletes custom category names you have created. It restores categories to Outlook's default.
/cleanclientrules	This starts Outlook, deleting all client-side rules.
/cleandmrecords	This deletes logging records that are saved when a manager or a delegate declines a meeting.
/cleanfinders	This removes search folders from Microsoft Exchange Server.
/cleanfreebusy	This clears and regenerates free/busy information and can be used only if you are using (and are connected to) your Exchange Server machine.
/cleanprofile	This removes invalid profile information and re-creates the registry where applicable.
/cleanreminders	This clears and regenerates reminders.
/cleanroamedprefs	All roamed preferences are deleted and copied from the local settings on the computer where this switch is used. This includes the roaming settings for reminders, free/busy grid, working hours, calendar publishing, and RSS rules.
/cleanrules	This starts Outlook and deletes client-based and server-based rules.
/cleanserverrules	This starts Outlook and deletes server-based rules.
/cleansharing	This removes RSS, Internet Calendar, and SharePoint subscriptions from Account Settings, leaving previously downloaded content. You can use this if you cannot delete these subscriptions from inside Outlook.
/cleansniff	This overrides programmatic lockout, determining which computers, if running Outlook simultaneously, will process meeting items. The lockout process helps prevent duplicate reminder messages. This switch clears this lockout.

Continued

Table 10-1. *Continued*

Switch	Description of Functionality
/cleansubscriptions	This deletes subscription messages and properties for subscription features.
/cleanviews	This restores default views with any custom views being lost.
/embedding	This opens a specified message file (.msg) as OLE embedding and can also be used without command-line parameters for a standard OLE cocreate.
/f *msgfilename*	This opens the specified message file (.msg) or Microsoft Office saved search (.oss).
/finder	This opens the Advanced Find dialog box.
/firstrun	This starts Outlook as if it were run for the first time.
/hol *holfilename*	This opens a specified .hol file.
/ical *icsfilename*	This opens a specified .ics file.
/importprf *prffilename*	This starts Outlook and opens or imports a defined MAPI profile (*.prf). If Outlook is already open, this switch will queue the profile to be imported the next time Outlook starts.
/launchtraininghelp *assetid*	This opens a Help window with the Help topic specified in assetid displayed.
/m *emailname*	This provides a way to add an email name to the item, working in conjunction with the /c command-line parameter.
/nocustomize	This starts Outlook without loading customized toolbars.
/noextensions	This starts Outlook with extensions off but listed as available in the Add-In Manager.
/nopreview	This starts Outlook with the Reading pane switched off.
/p *msgfilename*	This prints the specified message (.msg file).
/profile *profilename*	This loads the specified profile. If your profile name contains a space, enclose the profile name in quotation marks (" ").
/profiles	This opens the Choose Profile dialog box regardless of the Options setting on the Tools menu.
/recycle	This starts Outlook using an existing Outlook window if one exists. This is used in combination with /explorer or /folder.

Switch	Description of Functionality
/remigratecategories	This starts Outlook and upgrades colors and follow-up flags to Office Outlook 2007 color categories, upgrades calendar labels to Office Outlook 2007 color categories, and adds all categories used on non-mail items into the Master Category List.
/resetfolders	This restores missing folders at the default delivery location.
/resetfoldernames	This resets folder names (such as Inbox or Sent Items) to Outlook's default.
/resetformregions	This empties the form cache and reloads the form region definitions from the Windows registry.
/resetnavpane	This clears and regenerates the Navigation pane for the current user's profile.
/resetsearchcriteria	This resets all Instant Search criteria so that the default set of criteria is shown in each module.
/resetsharedfolders	This removes all shared folders from the Navigation pane.
/resettodobar	This clears and regenerates the To-Do Bar task list for the current profile.
/rpcdiag	This opens Outlook and displays the Remote Procedure Call (RPC) Connection Status dialog box.
/safe	This starts Outlook without Microsoft Exchange Server Client Extensions (ECE), the Reading pane, or toolbar customizations. Component Object Model (COM) add-ins are turned off.
/safe:1	This starts Outlook with the Reading pane off.
/safe:3	This starts Outlook with Microsoft Exchange Server Client Extensions (ECE) turned off but listed in the Add-In Manager. Component Object Model (COM) add-ins are turned off.
/safe:4	This starts Outlook without loading customized toolbars.
/select *foldername*	This opens the specified folder in a new window.
/sniff	This starts Outlook and forces a detection of new meeting requests in the Inbox, adding them to the calendar.
/t *oftfilename*	This opens the specified .oft file.
/v *vcffilename*	This opens the specified .vcf file.
/vcal *vcsfilename*	This opens the specified .vcs file.
/x *xnkfilename*	This opens the specified .xnk file.

Using Profiles

When you start Outlook regularly, without using any command-line switches, you are prompted to select the profile you want to use if you have more than one defined.

> **NOTE** In some circumstances, it's worth having multiple profiles defined to differentiate between your various ways of working, such as the difference between work and personal email, with each profile having separate accounts and configuration settings depending on the way you collect and process information in that context.

To see the profiles you have already set up on your system, from the Start menu right-click the E-mail icon, and select Properties. In the Mail Setup – Outlook dialog box, select Show Profiles, and then you'll see the Mail dialog box shown in Figure 10-1.

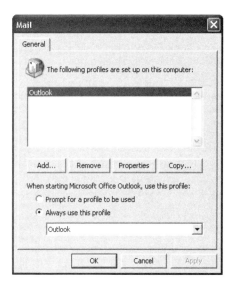

Figure 10-1. Manage Outlook profiles.

The default profile, when Outlook is started for the first time, is Outlook. This profile is loaded automatically when you log in to Outlook, and you don't need to do anything unless you need to create an alternative. To create a new profile, click the Add button, and then in the dialog box shown in Figure 10-2, type a meaningful name for the new profile. Finally, click OK.

Figure 10-2. Give an alternative profile a meaningful name that defines its purpose.

When you click OK, you have the option of adding a new email account to this profile. If you select Manually Configure Server Settings or Additional Server Types in the Add New E-mail Account Wizard, you can run through the usual method for adding new accounts. When you finish adding accounts to the new profile, click Finish, and you'll now see the new profile in the Mail dialog box, shown in Figure 10-3.

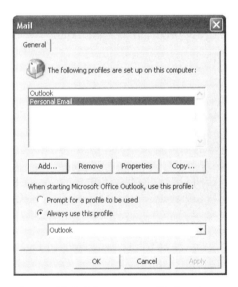

Figure 10-3. The new profile has been added to the list.

If you want to add more accounts to the profile, highlight the one you are interested in modifying, and then click Properties.

If you select Prompt for a Profile to Be Used, Outlook will always start by asking which profile you want to use for the ensuing session, allowing you to select from a drop-down list. If you would rather have Outlook always start without prompting, even when you have multiple profiles, select Always Use This Profile; then in the future, to switch profiles, select the one you would like to always start with in the drop-down list.

Using RUNAS with outlook.exe

The RUNAS command was introduced in Windows 2000 and brings to Windows Vista the ability to run an application from your logged-in user session as another user by authenticating the alternative account credentials from your current logon session. In this way, you can open Outlook as another user using the RUNAS command without having to log off.

The syntax for the RUNAS command is as follows:

```
RUNAS [/profile] [/env] [/netonly] /user:<username> program
```

The profile parameter forces the user's profile to be loaded and should be included; env uses the current user's environment (rather than the alternative account's profile) and is not so applicable for Outlook in this context. netonly is used only for remote access users and is probably not applicable in the context of Outlook. You must specify the <username>, and you will be prompted for the user's password before the program can be run. Finally, type the program name, in this case outlook.exe, specifying the full path and any appropriate command-line switches you want used.

Customizing Outlook Views

In Outlook, a *view* determines how the information in a specific area of functionality, such as in the Mail, Calendar, or Contacts folder, is displayed on the screen. The way the information is laid out for you when you first use Outlook follows the pattern of the standard views, but if these standard views don't quite meet your needs, you can customize all of them in some way or another.

Take, for example, the Inbox view in the Mail folder, as shown in Figure 10-4. The rest of this section looks at customizing the Inbox; however, each of the other Outlook folders are customized in the same way, so we won't repeat this explanation for the Calendar, Contacts, Notes, and Tasks folders.

You are probably aware by now that each individual item in Outlook contains a long list of various fields associated with it. There is no way to show all of these fields simultaneously on the screen, so Microsoft has selected the default set to be what it believes are the most useful out of the bunch.

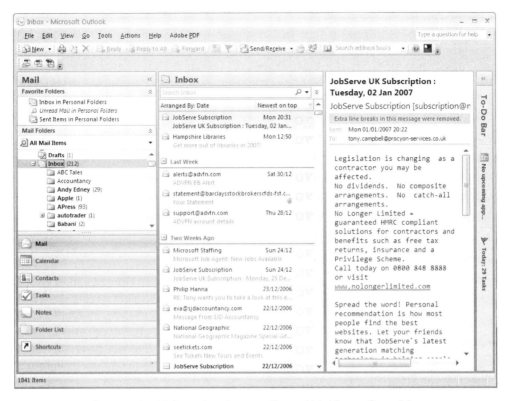

Figure 10-4. The standard Inbox view is versatile and highly configurable.

To change the default view, you need to be aware of a couple of menu choices. Then it's a simple matter of experimenting with the available fields to make the view do what you want, as follows:

- You can configure the Reading pane to be on the right of the inbox, beneath the inbox, or switched off if you no longer require it. To change the way the Reading pane appears, click View ➤ Reading Pane, and then select from Right, Bottom, or Off.

TIP Outlook behaves differently depending on the position of the Reading pane on the screen. If you have it on the right side of the inbox, you get, by default, two columns that you can use to order the information you see on the screen. However, if you switch off the Reading pane or move it to the bottom of the Inbox, you will notice more columns appear. If you right-click the columns with the Reading pane in either of these two states, you can select Field Chooser from the content menu. To add any of the fields shown in the Field Chooser to your inbox, it's a simple matter of dragging them from the Field Choose dialog box onto the inbox header. The new column will appear in the list in the position to which you drag it. If you want to move a column to a different location, again, it's a simple matter of dragging and dropping.

- By default, Outlook will always show two columns above the inbox: Arranged By Date and Newest on Top. This arrangement will ensure your most recent emails are always shown on top. Nevertheless, you can alter the columns by clicking View ➤ Arrange By and then selecting from Date, Conversation, From, To, Categories, Flag: Start Date, Flag: Due Date, Size, Subject, Type, Attachments, E-mail Account, and Importance. All of these speak for themselves as attributes, and you can use each in its own right for different ways of sorting the contents of your inbox. For example, to quickly find emails from a certain contact, reorder the inbox by From, and you'll see the entire set of emails ordered alphabetically by sender.

- If you click View ➤ Arrange By, you can toggle the Show in Groups feature. This groups like items relevant to the attribute you have selected for Arrange By. For example, grouping items arranged by Date will quickly show you all items that arrived today, yesterday, last week, two weeks ago, three weeks ago, last month, and older. If you arrange the items by From, the groupings change to the name of the sender.

- If you are using groups, clicking View ➤ Expand/Collapse Groups allows you to select the way you'd like to see the groups represented, such as having them all collapsed, as shown in Figure 10-5.

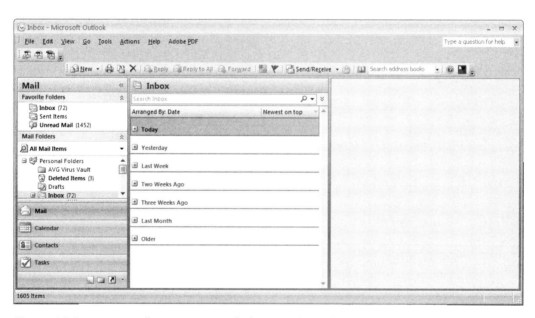

Figure 10-5. You can collapse groups to help you select which email you want to view.

- AutoPreview (toggled on or off from the View menu) will display the first few lines of text from an email beneath the sender's name or address and the subject in the inbox. This allows you to quickly scan down the inbox for a particular message without having to individually open each one.

- If you click View ➤ Current View, you'll see eight preset views you can switch to for your email. The default, Messages, has the inbox in the middle and the Reading pane on the right side. If you switch to one of the other presets, you'll see the messages ordered in that way; for example, Unread Messages in This Folder will display only email messages that are marked as Unread.

NOTE You can also manipulate how the Navigation pane (on the far left of the screen) and the To-Do Bar (on the far right of the screen) look, ranging from turning these features off completely to having them prevalent on the interface. To change how the Navigation pane and To-Do Bar are displayed, click View, and then select the appropriate options from the Navigation pane and To-Do Bar menus.

On top of this simple customization, you can further configure the columns shown on the screen using the Format Column window, available through View ➤ Current View ➤ Format Columns, as shown in Figure 10-6.

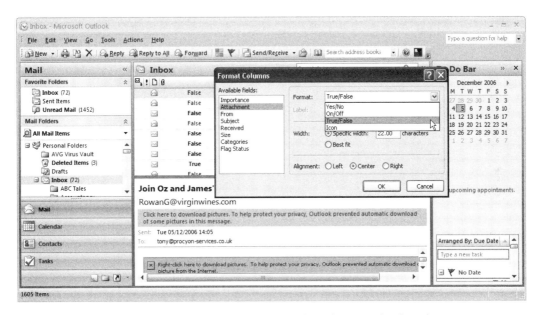

Figure 10-6. Format how the columns displayed in the inbox are displayed.

A good example of changing how information is displayed in a typical field column is under the Attachment field; you can switch the data format displayed from the standard paperclip icon to be True/False, Yes/No, or On/Off, depending on which you find more suitable. These formatting changes are available across the board on many of the column settings. It's a matter of looking for formats and alignments that best suit your needs and configuring the view appropriately.

NOTE Using the Format Columns window, you can change the alignment of a column displayed in the inbox from being left-aligned by default to being either right-aligned or centered.

Using Outlook Today

Outlook Today is feature of Outlook used to preview what you should expect during the rest of the day. To see the Outlook Today screen, as shown in Figure 10-7, you must click the top level of your Exchange Server account or your Personal Folders mail folders. Outlook Today will be displayed on the right side of the interface where you'd expect to see your inbox and the Reading pane.

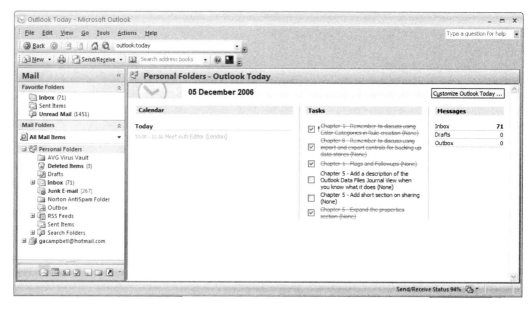

Figure 10-7. Outlook Today shows a preview of the rest of the day's activities.

The default Outlook Today screen shows three distinct columns: Calendar, Tasks, and Messages. You'll see all calendar items pertaining to appointments for that day, any outstanding tasks that are yet to be completed, and a summary of your email (totals for unread items in your inbox, any draft emails you've saved, and what's sitting in your outbox).

You can easily customize what you see in Outlook Today by clicking the Customize Outlook Today button on the top-right corner of the screen, as shown in Figure 10-8.

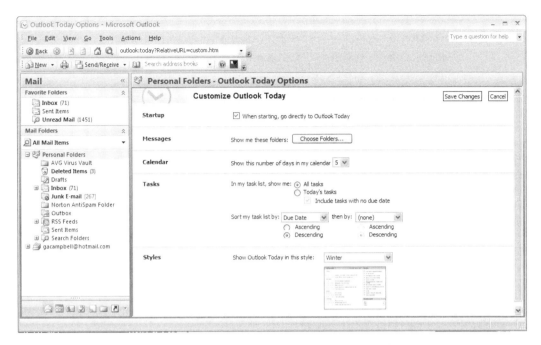

Figure 10-8. Customize Outlook Today for a more personal view of what's happening.

At the top of the customization screen, you'll see the Startup setting called When Starting, Go Directly to Outlook Today. If this is selected, each time you start Outlook, you will see Outlook Today automatically. Deselecting this checkbox will mean Outlook starts up in your inbox. If you click Choose Folders next to the Messages setting, you can select which folders are displayed on the Outlook Today page under the Messages column (remember the default was Inbox, Drafts, and Outbox, but you can have whichever folders you like).

You can change the number of days the Calendar column will show, so instead of the default of the next five days, you could limit it strictly to today, or you could look two weeks ahead. It's also possible to alter the way tasks are displayed, with all outstanding tasks shown by default, but you can change this to show today's tasks only and, if necessary, include tasks with no due date attached. There are various preferences for how your tasks will be displayed, how you sort them, and whether this is in ascending or descending order.

Lastly, you can apply an alternative style to Outlook Today in case you don't like the default. The choices are as follows:

Standard: This is the default setting with three columns for calendar appointments, tasks, and messages.

Standard (two column): This option places the messages and tasks together on the right side of the screen with more space devoted to the calendar.

Standard (one column): This stacks the three views in one column with the calendar at the top, tasks in the middle, and messages on the bottom.

Summer: The summer scheme reverts Outlook today to three columns but softens the color scheme with a gentle yellow background.

Winter: Lastly, the winter scheme changes the colors to be colder, including only whites and blues, without the nice summery yellows from the default and summer views.

Using Advanced Techniques for Customizing Views

You can perform advanced customization of Outlook views in two ways:

- Altering a standard view (the ones already discussed)
- Creating a new one from scratch

To create a new view based on an existing one, the following procedure should help:

1. Change to the view you'd like to customize, and then click View ➤ Arrange By ➤ Custom. You'll see the Customize View: Messages dialog box, as shown in Figure 10-9.

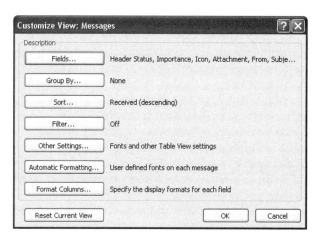

Figure 10-9. Click each customizable feature in turn, and create a bespoke view for your needs.

2. Use the buttons to customize the functionality of the view in the way you need; for example, if you want to add or remove columns, click the Fields button, and you'll see the Show Fields dialog box, as shown in Figure 10-10.

Figure 10-10. Add or remove columns in your view using the Show Fields dialog box.

3. When you finish configuring your view, close the Customize View: <current view> screen by clicking OK, and then click View ➤ Current View ➤ Define Views.

4. When you see the Custom View Organizer, as shown in Figure 10-11, highlight <Current view settings>, and then click Copy.

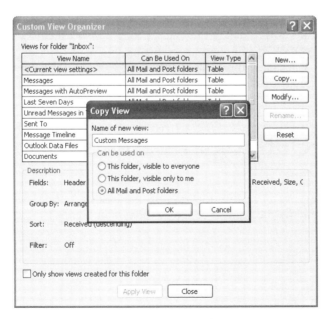

Figure 10-11. Use your current settings to create a new custom view.

5. Type a meaningful name for your new view, select how this folder can be used, and then click OK.

6. If you want to reset the view you customized to its original settings, highlight the original view in the Custom View Organizer, and then click Reset.

To create a view from scratch, select New in the Custom View Organizer, give the view a meaningful name, and then select its type from the list, as shown in Figure 10-12.

Figure 10-12. Select the type of view you are creating.

All you have to do now is define the fields, grouping, sort methods, and so on, that you would do usually if you were customizing one of the standard views. To switch to your new view, click the View menu, select Current View, and then select your custom view from the list.

Configuring Outlook Preferences

You can manage basic functionality for each of Outlook's capabilities through the Tools ➤ Options menu on the Preferences tab, as shown in Figure 10-13.

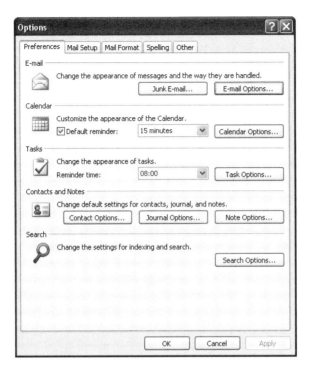

Figure 10-13. Use the Preferences tab to manage the functionality of Outlook's main features.

From here, you can modify the basic operation of all of Outlook's features by clicking the relevant button.

Email Options

You can change how Outlook performs basic messaging functions such as whether to save a copy of each message you send to the Sent Items folder. Further advanced options allow you to specify the time between automatically saving items (the default is three minutes) and how Outlook behaves when it receives an email. You can also modify how Outlook handles junk email by modifying the settings of the junk email filter.

Calendar Options

Preferences for modifying the behavior of your calendar include how Outlook handles time zones, how you display free/busy time to others, and how the working week is defined; for example, you might start the work week on Sunday rather than Monday if you are a shift worker.

Tasks Options

These options are limited to changing color preferences for how overdue and completed tasks are displayed on the screen and how Outlook behaves regarding status reports for completed tasks and reminders for unfinished tasks.

Contact Options

Preferences available for modifying the behavior of contacts are limited to how the contact's name is displayed (that is, the order of the first, last, and middle names) and how Outlook handles contacts with duplicate names.

Journal Options

These options are specifically for defining which items are automatically recorded in your Journal, which contacts the Journal records these items against, and which Office applications outside the remit of Outlook also have activity recorded.

Note Options

You can specify the default color and size of new notes as well as the font and point size of the text used within.

Search Options

These options are available to allow you to specify exactly which folders are automatically indexed by Outlook, how instant search reacts to you beginning to type a search query in the Search box, and whether to include items in the Deleted Items folder in the search.

CHAPTER 11

Security and Backup

As with all aspects of computing, security is high on the agenda for Outlook users. Threats are posed from a variety of sources, typically originating on the Internet, and exhibit themselves in the form of email-borne viruses, malicious scripts, and social-engineering lures that entice you into doing something you shouldn't.

Previous versions of Outlook were criticized for having a plethora of security vulnerabilities that were easily exploited through an arsenal of readily available mechanisms, but Outlook 2003 was certainly a bold and positive step in the right direction for mitigating those threats. Outlook 2007 builds upon the foundation of Outlook 2003 and introduces enhancements in areas such as content blocking and macro security.

Another great advantage of Outlook 2007 over previous versions is that you can access all security settings (mirrored across the rest of the Office suite) through a single unified interface called the Trust Center.

This chapter looks at the threats faced when you use Outlook in anger and how you go about using the Trust Center to bolster your defenses and mitigate the threats.

Introducing the Trust Center

The Trust Center is the primary interface for security-related matters in Outlook. To access the Trust Center, select Tools ➤ Trust Center. The following sections will step you through each of the options available in the Trust Center so you can get a feel for how you can best configure security to suit your own needs.

Trusted Publishers

A *trusted publisher* is a software development company that you are happy to have execute a macro, ActiveX control, or other such add-in on your system. If, for example, you have Adobe Systems registered as a trusted publisher, then you can use software from Adobe without concern (see Figure 11-1).

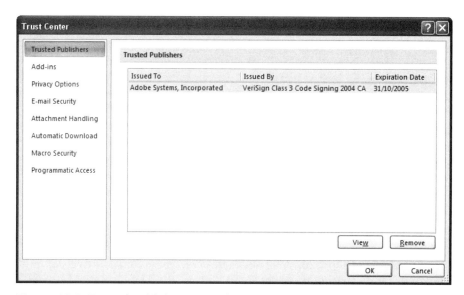

Figure 11-1. Trusted publishers are software vendors you trust to run code on your system.

To help you decide whether you can trust a publisher, you'll need to know who that publisher is and how that publisher can prove that it is trustworthy. Large companies, such as Adobe in this example, are easy to assess, but smaller companies that might produce an add-in that forms part of a bigger suite of software are harder to assess and can cause you concern.

Microsoft has created the following questions to help you assess the trustworthiness of a publisher:

- Is the code signed using a digital signature?
- Is the digital signature valid?
- Is the digital signature current?
- Was the certificate that is associated with the digital signature obtained from a trusted authority?
- Is the publisher who signed the code a trusted publisher?

With a quick explanation of what each of these questions means, you'll see that due diligence on publishers is not as onerous a task as it might appear at first glance.

A *digital signature* is an electronic stamp that can be applied to a piece of information or application in order to prove its authenticity. If the signature is demonstrated to be valid, you can assert that the file has not been tampered with. Obviously, the key to making this system work is in proving the validity of the signature. Luckily, a mechanism within the operating system's certificate management capability will help you do this; specifically, you can check the certificate used to create the signature against the issuing authority, and if the certificate is valid and current, you can assume that the signature is authentic.

> **NOTE** A *certificate authority* is an organization that specializes in providing certificate services to end users, including issuing and managing publishing certificates, email encryption certificates, or certificates used to sign your own certificate authority.

When you try to execute a piece of code within Outlook that does not meet all the aforementioned criteria, Outlook denies the execution of the code. Outlook will inform you that it has encountered a potentially unsafe piece of code and offers you the chance to check it. How Outlook reacts will depend entirely on how you have set your Macro Security settings, described in the next section.

To check that a publisher's certificate is valid, you can check the certificate of an existing publisher in the Trust Center, or if the publisher is as yet untrusted, you can opt to check the certificate in the dialog box that's displayed when you first try to execute the code.

From the Trust Center, do the following:

1. Highlight the publisher's name in the Issued To column, and then click View.

2. The certificate appears, focused on the General tab. Take note of whom the certificate was issued to, whom it was issued by, and the dates that the certificate are valid between. The Details tab will reveal the cryptographic aspects of the certificate, which, although interesting, probably won't mean that much to you. What's more important is the Certification Path tab, as shown in Figure 11-2.

Figure 11-2. Use the Certification Path tab to discover where the certificate originated.

3. Notice in this example that the certification path can be traced back to a Class 3 Public Primary CA owned by VeriSign. You can double-click any of the certificates listed on the Certification Path tab to view *their* validity and details, as shown in Figure 11-3.

Figure 11-3. Check the validity of each certificate in the chain to ensure trust is inherent.

If there is a problem in any way with a certificate, you'll see a white *x* in a red circle embossed over the certificate's name. If this is the case, check with the publisher about why the certificate is invalid or out-of-date—they may be able to issue you an up-to-date certificate that provides an unbroken chain of trust.

> **TIP** To add a new developer to the Trusted Publisher list, when the dialog box warning of the potentially unsafe code appears, you can instruct Outlook to add it to the Trusted Publisher list. To remove a publisher from the list, open the Trust Center, select Trusted Publishers, highlight the one you want to remove, and then click the Remove button.

Setting Add-in and Macro Security

Add-ins are clever extensions to Outlook's capability that leverage the inherent extensibility of the Outlook development environment.

To see a list of add-ins already installed on your system, open the Trust Center, and then select Add-ins on the left side of the screen. You'll see a list like the one shown in Figure 11-4.

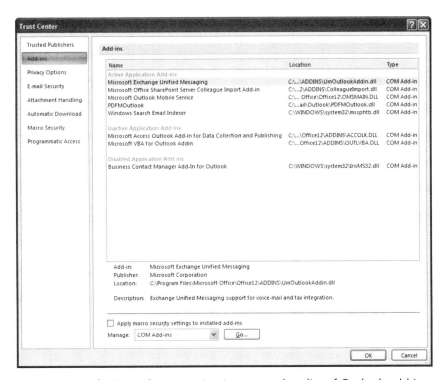

Figure 11-4. The Trust Center maintains a complete list of Outlook add-ins.

You can manage three distinct sections of add-ins, as follows:

- Active add-ins that are currently loaded into Outlook
- Inactive add-ins that are installed on your system but not yet loaded into Outlook
- Disabled add-ins where execution rights have been explicitly revoked

To install, remove, or enable disabled add-ins, in the Manage box at the bottom of the screen, select the add-in you are interested in changing, and then click Go. You have the option, with the COM Add-Ins item, to add or remove items from the list, or you can change the way an add-in is handled by checking or unchecking the selection box to determine how the add-in is treated when Outlook starts, as shown in Figure 11-5.

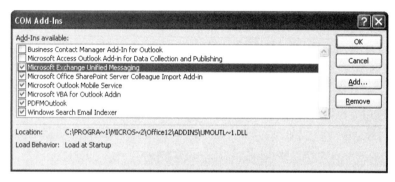

Figure 11-5. Add or remove COM add-ins from Outlook through the Trust Center.

From the Add-ins interface, open the Manage drop-down menu, select Disabled Items, and then click Go to reenable any add-ins that have previously been disabled, as shown in Figure 11-6.

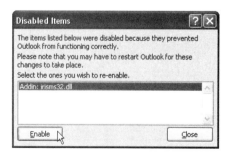

Figure 11-6. Enable add-ins through the Disabled Items dialog box

> **NOTE** You have the option of enabling an add-in for the current session only if you'd prefer not to install it permanently onto your system. You can do this when Outlook first encounters the add-in, and at this stage, you can opt to trust add-ins from this publisher all the time or to disable it if you are unsure of its intent.

By default Outlook will happily allow any add-in installed on the system to run. It is assumed you have authorized the add-in in the first place, so there is no reason to prohibit its running. However, you can limit this open approach to add-ins by instructing Outlook to run only those add-ins that have a valid digital signature associated with them. To do this, follow these steps:

1. In the Trust Center, click Macro Security.
2. Select Warnings for Signed Macros; All Unsigned Macros Are Disabled.
3. Now click Add-Ins.
4. Check the Apply Macro Security Settings to Installed Add-Ins checkbox.

From now on, all add-ins, whether they are installed on your system or not, are bound by the rules dictated within your Macro Security settings.

Other macro settings are as follows:

No Warnings and Disable All Macros: This is by far the most secure of the options available, but it seriously limits the functionality of any forms or templates.

Warnings for Signed Macros; All Unsigned Macros Are Disabled: This less restrictive option will still warn you when you are running a macro (although that macro must be signed), but it will block all access to macros that do not have a valid digital signature.

Warnings for All Macros: If you select this option, you will be informed that a macro is about to execute but Outlook will ignore whether or not the macro is digitally signed. All macros will be allowed as long as they are user authorized.

No Security Check for Macros (Not Recommended): This one is obvious. There is no security, and you won't receive any warnings. All macros will run automatically without prompting about whether they have a digital signature.

Introducing Privacy

Privacy describes the way you view personal and/or private information that you might not want to share with others. In Outlook, privacy relates to the control you have over Outlook's ability to perform specific tasks on the Internet that you might deem unacceptable, such as searching Office Online for new information that might be applicable to you or signing up for Microsoft's Customer Experience Improvement Program.

Figure 11-7 shows the privacy options available in Outlook.

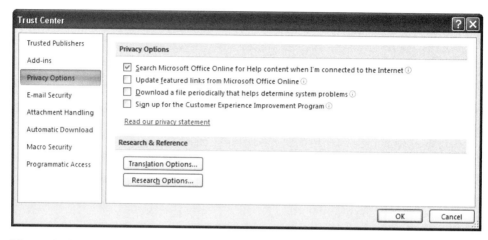

Figure 11-7. Privacy options available in Outlook

The privacy options available for configuration are as follows:

Search Microsoft Office Online for Help Content When I'm Connected to the Internet: This option means Outlook can connect to Office Online to get the most up-to-date Help content. It's important to realize that the entire content of the Help system is not downloaded to your computer if this option is checked; instead, only the article you are concerned with is downloaded.

Update Featured Links from Microsoft Office Online: This will download the most up-to-date featured templates to your system from Office Online.

Download a File Periodically That Helps Determine System Problems: This option allows a diagnostic file to be downloaded from Office Online so that if your system crashes, Office Diagnostics automatically runs to help fix the problem.

Sign Up for the Customer Experience Improvement Program: The Customer Experience Improvement Program helps Microsoft improve its products. If you decide to participate, information is automatically collected from your computer, such as error messages, the kind of system you are running, and whether your system is struggling to run any Microsoft software. This information is collected and sent to Microsoft once each day, although it's with the understanding that all the information sent to Microsoft will remain completely anonymous.

Setting Up Email Security

If you take a look at the E-mail Security settings in the Trust Center, you'll see that this section primarily deals with the use of digital certificates for encrypting and signing email.

A *digital certificate* is a security mechanism that connects your user ID to a pair of encryption keys (very large prime numbers); one is known as your *private* key, and the other is known as your *public* key.

The private key is known only to you, whereas the public key is freely distributed to whomever needs it. When you encrypt something using this mechanism, you perform what's known as a *one-way* function on the data using one of the keys, and the only way to decrypt it is to use the other key. The same key cannot be used to encrypt and decrypt the same piece of data (which is why it's called a *one-way* function).

The mathematics that underpin how this system works are largely unimportant (if you are really interested in finding out more about how public key cryptography works, visit http://www.entrust.com/pki.htm), but rest assured it is the most cryptographically strong way of ensuring your communications are safe, secure, and not tampered with.

> **NOTE** You'll often hear digital signatures mentioned in the same breath as digital certificates, but it's worth realizing the difference between the two. A digital signature uses a mathematical function to calculate a unique number based on the content of the message. This function is known as a *hashing function* and will produce a very different result if even a single bit in the original file is modified. Digital signatures protect the integrity of items you send and also prove they originated from you. If you digitally sign an email, there is no way it can be intercepted and modified by an intermediary, because the payload of the email will change, and the hash will change. When you use Outlook to create a signed email, Outlook first hashes it to produce the numerical value (known as the *message digest*), and then it uses your private key to encrypt that hash. This way, the recipient of the email uses your public key to verify the signature came from you and then runs the hash function against the message content to prove it has not been modified.

Interestingly, when you want to send an encrypted message, it's different from how you send a signed message (Outlook takes care of this for you so there's no need to fret), and these two mechanisms each provide a slightly different security benefit.

If you digitally sign a message, you are gaining message integrity but not confidentiality, thus ensuring the message has not been modified. Encrypting a message provides confidentiality, meaning no one can intercept and read the message content.

This entire system works on the basis of everyone having free access to each person's digital certificate (containing the public key, the user ID, the validity dates, and so on), whilst the private keys remain private, known only to the individuals they are assigned. If a private key is suspected of being compromised in any way, it should be revoked, thus ending its life and ensuring it cannot be used again in the future.

Obtaining a Certificate

In the Trust Center's E-mail Security settings, shown in Figure 11-8, click the Get a Digital ID button. This opens Microsoft's Office Online Digital ID website where digital certificate providers, such as Comodo and VeriSign, offer their services. Personal certificates are sometimes free whereas business-use certificates come at a premium, so make sure you shop around to get the solution you require.

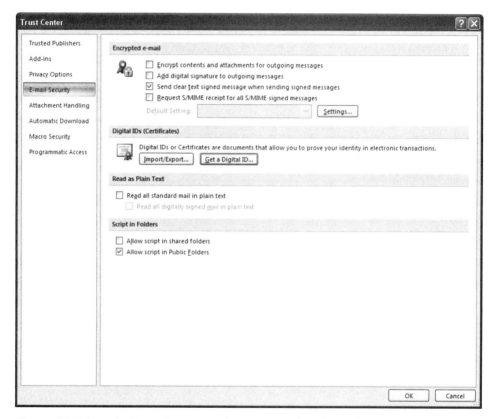

Figure 11-8. Use the Trust Center to obtain a new digital certificate for use in Outlook.

When you've followed the instructions from the vendor to install the certificate on your computer, you are ready to start sending both signed and encrypted messages. The certificate will now be listed in the Trust Center next to Default Setting.

Certificate Settings

You can perform various administrative functions on certificates using the Settings button available in the Trust Center. When you first click Settings, you'll see the dialog box shown in Figure 11-9.

Figure 11-9. Change the default behavior of your certificate settings using the Change Security Settings dialog box.

Starting at the top of the dialog box, the Security Settings Name defaults to My S/MIME Settings (<the email address in the certificate>). You can change this name if you want something that better describes the nature of this configuration.

The Cryptography Format option is set to S/MIME automatically; however, you can select Exchange Server Security from the drop-down list if you are using Microsoft Exchange Server to provide your protection. For a stand-alone system on a home network, leave this as S/MIME.

> **NOTE** Secure/Multipurpose Internet Mail Extensions (S/MIME) is a standard designed to allow public key encryption techniques to be used with MIME email formatting. MIME is the most popular email-formatting standard used on the Internet today, extending the Simple Mail Transfer Protocol (SMTP) beyond the basic 7-bit ASCII character to include nontext attachments and extended formatting. Most email sent using Outlook is formatted using the SMTP/MIME standard.

Default Security Setting for This Cryptographic Message Format makes the listed security settings the default for all the messages shown in the Cryptography Format list. Selecting Default Security Setting for All Cryptographic Messages applies the settings on both S/MIME-formatted and Exchange Server–formatted messages.

Security labels display relevant security information about a specific message, placing restrictions on the recipient when it comes to reading and forwarding that message. These labels are assigned through the security policy and are administratively controlled. Your system administrator in a business environment will supply these.

Click the New button to create a new array of security settings that you can subsequently switch to if you want to quickly select a new cryptographic format or a different certificate. Delete allows you to remove the currently open security profile.

Click the Password button to change the password assigned to security settings.

The Signing Certificate option is the certificate selected from your certificate store (a secure location within the operating system), and you can change it by clicking Choose. The Select Certificate dialog box, shown in Figure 11-10, shows the certificate store (in this case it contains only one certificate, used for both signing and encrypting). You can do the same selection process with the encryption certificate.

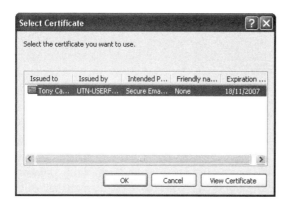

Figure 11-10. Outlook allows you to choose separate certificates for each cryptographic function.

You can select the Hash Algorithm and the Encryption Algorithm options from their respective drop-down lists, but the settings used by default (SHA1 and 3DES) are the most secure.

Finally, select the Send These Certificates with Signed Messages checkbox to ensure Outlook distributes your certificates to recipients who receive signed messages.

NOTE A digital certificate does not contain a private key, so you can rest assured that when you distribute a certificate to a recipient, all you are doing is letting that recipient have your public key, which is essential for decrypting the message digest on a signature.

Configuration in the Trust Center

The settings configured in the Trust Center will apply by default to all messages. They're at the top of the E-mail Security settings (refer to Figure 11-8), as follows:

Encrypt Contents and Attachments for Outgoing Messages: This ensures all messages are encrypted. When you encrypt a message for a recipient, you actually use that recipient's public key in the function. In this way, only that recipient can decrypt the message since she's the only one with access to the private key (mathematically bound to the public key).

Add Digital Signature to Outgoing Messages: This ensures all outbound messages are signed using the specified hash function (SHA1) and your private key. Your certificate will allow the recipient to test whether the message has been tampered with.

Send Clear Text Signed Message When Sending Signed Messages: This sends a digitally signed message to a recipient who does not use S/MIME. You should uncheck this box unless you encounter a problem because this is less secure. Most clients nowadays use S/MIME.

Request S/MIME Receipts for All S/MIME Signed Messages: This asks the recipient for a secure receipt when the message is opened and the signature verified. Outlook will automatically do this.

Processing Signed or Encrypted Messages

If someone sends you an email that has been digitally signed or encrypted, the message appears in your inbox with a small orange and yellow rosette emblazoned on the message icon (see Figure 11-11), signifying the use of digital certificate.

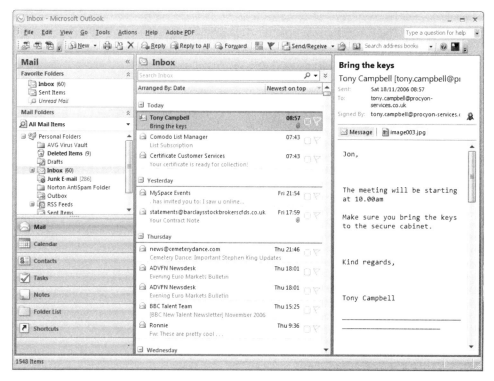

Figure 11-11. The message icon is emblazoned with a rosette signifying a digital certificate.

If you open the message, you'll see the same rosette on the right side of the message window (just above the message body), as shown in Figure 11-12. If you click the rosette in this window, a dialog box pops up to let you know whether the signature is valid (see Figure 11-13).

> **TIP** It's well worth selecting Warn Me About Errors in Digitally Signed E-mail Before Message Opens to give you the option to not open a message that might have been tampered with. Since the email might contain malicious code or scripts, you might make it policy to delete any message with an invalid signature.

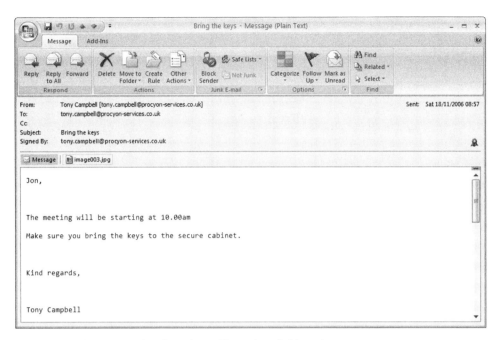

Figure 11-12. Access the digital certificate by clicking the rosette.

Figure 11-13. Clicking the rosette will expose whether the certificate is valid.

Clicking the Details button will expose the Message Security Properties dialog box, as shown in Figure 11-14. When you receive a message from a trusted recipient, you must add their certificate to your trusted list. To do this, highlight the Signer line in the Message Security Properties dialog box, and then click Edit Trust.

Figure 11-14. The Message Security Properties
dialog box shows the certificate's trust path
for the message.

When you view the Trust tab, shown in Figure 11-15, you'll see that the system is set to Inherit Trust from Issuer. This is used when the certificate comes from a commercial certificate authority that you can inherently trust, such as VeriSign, or from an enterprise authority such as one run by your own organization. If you opt to select Explicitly Trust This Certificate, you are instructing Outlook to place trust in emails signed using this certificate even when you can't establish a trust chain to an issuing authority. Use this option only when you are sure you can trust this certificate. Finally, selecting Explicitly Don't Trust this Certificate will force Outlook to block messages signed with this certificate even when trust can be established through a direct path to a trusted authority.

Figure 11-15. Establish the level of trust you have in a certificate.

You can opt to view details about any of the certificates in the trusted path by highlighting the certificate and selecting View Details.

Signing and Encrypting Emails

Before you can send an encrypted email to a recipient, you will need to obtain that person's certificate. This will store the recipient's public key in your system to use in encrypting emails to that person.

By far the best way to get your certificate to another user, or for them to send their certificate to you, is to construct a blank message, digitally sign it, and send it. A digital signature automatically appends the certificate to the message since it is required by the recipient to decrypt the message digest before the signature can be checked.

When you receive a signed email message, you must add that person to your Address Book in order to store their certificate. To do this, right-click the contact's name in the From field of the email, and then select Add to Outlook Contacts. This will open a new Outlook Contact window, as shown in Figure 11-16, with the Certificates button displayed at the top of the screen in the Show category on the Ribbon. Fill in the contact information as usual, and then click the Certificates button.

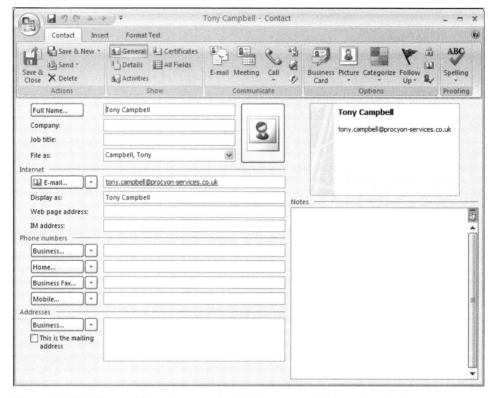

Figure 11-16. The certificate is stored with the contact information in the Address Book.

You can view this contact's certificate by highlighting the appropriate entry in the list and clicking Properties.

Sending an encrypted or signed message to a recipient is easy (once you've done everything previously covered here); do the following:

1. Click New, and select Mail Message as you would if you were composing a regular email.

2. Click the Sign button or the Encrypt button (or both) in the Options category on the Ribbon, as shown in Figure 11-17. This will add the appropriate signature or encryption to the message and apply it when you click Send.

3. If a problem occurs and you cannot, for example, encrypt the message because a certificate is not present for the recipient, you'll see the error message shown in Figure 11-18. In this case you have the option to send the message without encryption, although it will still be signed because this uses your own certificate and does not rely on you having the recipient's certificate in advance.

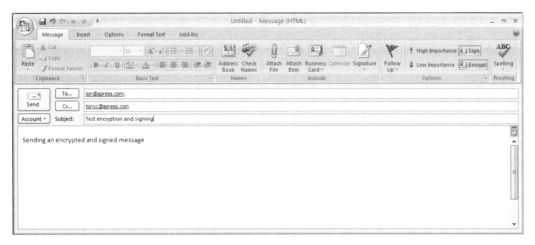

Figure 11-17. Use the Sign and Encrypt buttons on the Ribbon to sign and encrypt emails.

Figure 11-18. An error message appears if the message cannot be encrypted.

> **NOTE** If you are using an Exchange Server as your messaging server, it will handle certificate distribution for you automatically so you don't have to swap certificates with other Exchange users within your organization. When you receive an encrypted message from another user, you will not see the message body in the Preview pane; instead, you'll see a message instructing you that the email is encrypted. Outlook must process the message before it can be read, and to do this, you must completely open the message.

Making Attachments Secure

Many email messages contain attachments in the form of Office application files such as Word documents, Access databases, or PowerPoint presentations. You can attach any file you like to an email, and the same goes for executable code and script files.

Attachments can, however, pose a threat to your system since email-borne viruses and worms come in the form of an email attachment—it's almost the perfect vector to get into your system. It's quick, it's easy to bulk send, and it can be wrapped up in a social engineering package that can entice you to open the file where usually you'd be cautious.

In many cases something that appears innocent may well be hiding a malicious payload, such as the notorious I Love You virus that circulated the globe relying on people wondering who could be their secret admirer.

When you receive a message with an attachment, you can preview that attachment before opening it fully. To do this, you will need to have a piece of software called a *previewer* installed. These are available from Office Online (you get a link presented to you when you try to preview an attachment that has no installed previewer).

To preview a message attachment, right-click the attachment in the Preview pane, and select Preview. If you don't have a previewer installed, you'll see the message in Figure 11-19.

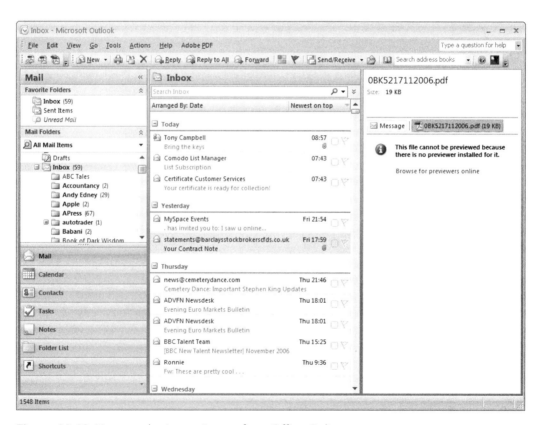

Figure 11-19. You can obtain previewers from Office Online.

NOTE At the time of writing, no previewers were available for files outside the Office suite. Adobe .pdf files, in this case, cannot be previewed.

If you try to preview a file that has an installed previewer, you'll see a warning that confirms your intention is to preview the file. If you don't want to see the warning in the future, uncheck Always Warn Before Previewing This Type of File.

If you switch to the Trust Center and select Attachment Handling, you'll see the screen shown in Figure 11-20.

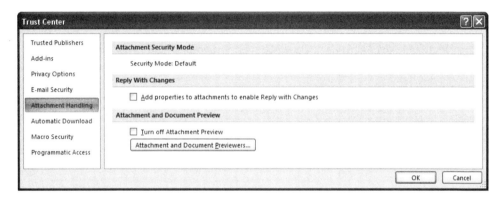

Figure 11-20. You can configure the way Outlook handles attachments in the Trust Center.

Get a list of the previewers already installed on your system by clicking Attachment and Document Previewers.

If you select Turn Off Attachment Preview, Outlook will no longer offer the option of previewing attachments in the Preview pane, but to make this operational, you'll have to close Outlook and start it again. If you've done this, the Preview option on the attachment context menu is removed.

Enabling Automatic Download and Content Blocking

You can configure how Outlook handles embedded content within HTML messages through the Trust Center. If you open the Trust Center and click the Automatic Download button, you'll see the screen shown in Figure 11-21.

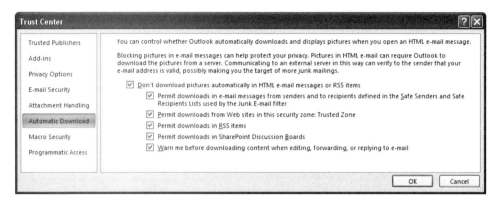

Figure 11-21. Automatic download settings determine how Outlook handles embedded content.

By blocking these sorts of content by default, Outlook is playing things extremely safe. By doing this, you are protected from malicious code and scripting that can be embedded within HTML objects that would inherently be executed if left to their own devices. The options you have for controlling the automatic download of embedded objects are as follows:

Don't Download Pictures Automatically in HTML E-mail Messages or RSS Items: By default this is checked. If you uncheck this overarching setting, Outlook will automatically download all the content embedded in emails; however, this is potentially unsafe, and we don't recommend it. Leaving it checked lets you have finer-grained control over the rest of the settings.

Permit Downloads in E-mail Messages from Senders and to Recipients Defined in the Safe Senders and Safe Recipients Lists Used by the Junk E-mail Filter: If recipients and senders are marked as safe in your junk email settings, content will automatically be downloaded.

Permit Downloads from Web Sites in This Security Zone: *Trusted Zone*: If you have added the targets for links in email to your Trusted Zone in Internet Explorer, the content can be trusted and will be automatically downloaded.

Permit Downloads in RSS Items: Some RSS feeds rely on content being downloaded, so if this is the case, enable it.

Permit Downloads in SharePoint Discussion Boards: Since SharePoint is a private web solution for business, it can be assumed to be trusted. This setting allows SharePoint resident data to be downloaded.

Warn Me Before Downloading Content When Editing, Forwarding or Replying to E-mail: This instructs Outlook to present a warning message before allowing content to be downloaded when you are replying to or forwarding a message containing such content.

If an email turns up containing content you have instructed Outlook to block, the email will appear malformed in the Preview pane with what appears to be pictures and content missing replaced by white squares with red *x*'s inside. You can access the content if you believe it to be safe by right-clicking one of the red *x*'s and selecting Download Pictures from the context menu.

Some attachments are considered potential virus threats and will always be blocked by Outlook. These files are executable files such as .exe and .vbs. In the case where you are creating an email with an attachment file considered unsafe by Outlook, you will be told that it is potentially unsafe and that other Outlook users will be unable to open it.

> **TIP** To send an attachment with a file type that is usually blocked, try zipping it first. Since these compressed files are not immediately executable until they are uncompressed, there is less risk of accidental execution; therefore, Outlook will permit these to pass through the filter.

Setting Up Information Rights Management

Information rights management (IRM) allows you to specify special access restrictions on emails (and other Office content) so you can impose more rigorous control over what recipients can do with the information. For example, you might want a user to read a piece of information you send to her, but you may not want her to print it out or alter it. This is what IRM can help you achieve; however, at this stage of the technology's maturity, there are still many, many ways to circumnavigate the protection; therefore, you should think of IRM as an extra layer rather than the be-all and end-all of security.

To enable IRM on your computer, you'll have to download the latest version of the Windows Rights Management Services client to your computer from Microsoft's website, as shown in Figure 11-22.

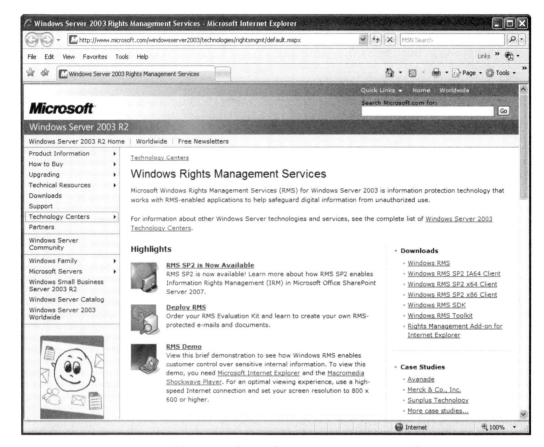

Figure 11-22. Use IRM to add an extra layer of protection to your overall system security.

The link to the website is as follows: `http://www.microsoft.com/windowsserver2003/technologies/rightsmgmt/default.mspx`.

When you receive a message that has been IRM protected, you will see a message in the InfoBar telling you the rights that have been applied to this message.

CHAPTER **12**

Outlook Outside the Office (or Home)

According to several statistics available in late summer 2006, sales of notebook computers have surpassed sales of more traditional desktop computers for nearly two years. So, there's a good probability that you are using, or will be using, Outlook 2007 on a laptop and that you'll be using Outlook away from your office or home base.

If your mail comes to an Exchange Server system, this scenario is particularly interesting, because it poses a question: how do you connect to Exchange Server remotely? How do you use Outlook without a connection? In this chapter, we'll cover offline folders, the Remote Mail mode, RPC over the Internet, and Cached Exchange Mode, which are all features designed to improve your experience using Outlook away from the office.

Using Offline Folders

Offline folders are key, as you might expect, to working with Outlook offline. If you don't have a set of offline folders preconfigured before you start Outlook without a network connection, Outlook will not be able to launch. Offline folders are simply stored in one file on your hard disk, with an .ost extension; this file is associated with the Exchange Server account in Outlook. You will not be able to see the offline folders when working within the Outlook user interface; the program uses them seamlessly without presenting them in your folder list.

> **NOTE** If you use Cached Exchange Mode, covered later in the "Using Cached Exchange Mode" section, Outlook creates the offline folders file automatically. You don't need to do anything.

If you need to manually create an offline folders file, do the following:

1. Select Tools ➤ Account Settings.
2. Select the Exchange Server account, and click the Change button.
3. Click the More Settings button.
4. Navigate to the Advanced tab.
5. Click the Offline Folder File Settings button.
6. The Offline Folder file Settings dialog box appears, as shown in Figure 12-1. In the File box, enter the location for the OST file.

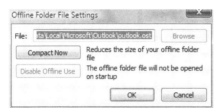

Figure 12-1. The Offline Folder File Settings dialog box

7. Click OK.
8. Click the Enable Offline Use button, and click OK.

Once you've created the file, you need to perform synchronization with the Exchange Server machine on your network. Make sure you're connected to the network that the Exchange Server machine resides on, and then within Outlook, select Tools ➤ Send/Receive, and pick the Microsoft Exchange Server account. The synchronization could take an hour or more, depending on the size of your mailbox

If you have a pretty big mailbox, chances are you have a lot of deleted files as well. Unfortunately, Outlook doesn't always reclaim space used by items deleted from the offline cache of your mailbox, so if you're low on disk space, consider clicking the Compact Now button in the Offline Folder File Settings box (the one shown in Figure 12-1). This will reclaim the wasted space and give you some free disk space back.

Using RPC Over HTTP

Previously, the ability to use Outlook remotely required a VPN connection. And although VPNs aren't necessarily bad, they are an additional level of complexity and add another layer of support required for mobile users. And a lot of times, from remote locations, firewalls restrict your ability to initiate an outbound VPN connection. (Some hotels are paranoid, and this can be frustrating.)

With these issues and problems in mind, Microsoft set out when it designed Exchange Server 2003 to offer a better way to connect Outlook to the business network when you are away from the office. Microsoft came up with RPC over HTTP, which essentially is a technical term that refers to one protocol that Outlook uses extensively and that is wrapped up in HTTP, the standard protocol used over the Web. Basically, HTTP acts as a capsule and encases Remote Procedure Call (RPC) transmissions. The advantages of this are twofold: first, there is no special configuration required on the client end, like a VPN connection profile; second, you can use Outlook from just about anywhere that allows web access. Although firewalls range in paranoia, most of them allow for standard outbound access on port 80 or 443.

There are a few initial requirements when setting up your clients to use the RPC over HTTP capabilities in Outlook. For one, make sure you're running Windows XP Service Pack 2—there's really no reason not to be, and support for Service Pack 1 will end by the time this book is in print.

Once you've found the systems that are up to that baseline, the next step is to install your Exchange Server's security certificate on each of these systems. This step basically tells each system to trust that the server is who it says it is and to not wonder whether the server is actually a rogue machine pretending to be your server with the intent to steal passwords, confidential information, and other sensitive material. To do this, you should open Internet Explorer and type the full Internet name of your Exchange Server computer (such as http://exchange.beyondthemanual.com). If you get a security warning, click the View Certificate button, click the Install Certificate button, and then follow the simple instructions from that point. Now, your computer automatically trusts your server, and you won't receive the security warnings anymore.

If you are not able to view the certificate in Internet Explorer, then you may need to get your network administrator to send you the certificate over email or through removable media.

It's now time to configure Outlook to use RPC over HTTP. Follow these steps:

1. On the client computer, make sure Outlook is closed.
2. Open the Control Panel from the Start menu.
3. Double-click the Mail applet. (You may have to switch to Classic view to see the icon.)
4. Click the E-mail Accounts button in the Mail Setup window.
5. Click View or Change Existing E-mail Accounts, and then click Next.
6. The E-mail Accounts screen appears. Select Microsoft Exchange Server, and then click the Change button.
7. Make sure your local server name, not the full Internet name, appears in the Microsoft Exchange Server field. Then, type your username in the User Name box, as shown in Figure 12-2.

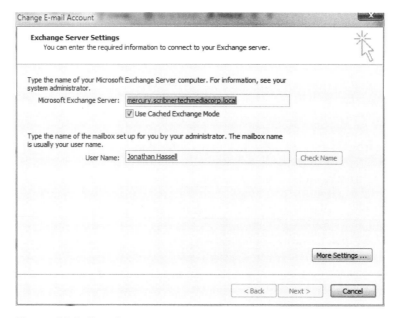

Figure 12-2. Entering server names

8. Click the More Settings button.

9. Navigate to the Connection tab.

10. Select the Connect to My Exchange Mailbox Using HTTP box at the bottom of the screen, and then click the Exchange Proxy Settings button.

11. The dialog box in Figure 12-3 appears. Type your Exchange Server's full Internet address in the Use This URL to Connect to My Proxy Server for Exchange field.

12. Check the Connect Using SSL Only box if your Exchange Server supports it. You'll want this to ensure your transmissions with Exchange Server are secure via SSL encryption. Check with your administrator.

13. Select Mutually Authenticate the Session When Connecting with SSL if your Exchange Server supports it.

14. Type the following in the Principal Name for Proxy Server field: **msstd: full_Internet_address**. Replace "full_Internet_address" with the full Internet address of your SBS server. Make sure there are no spaces in this field.

15. For the best results, select On Slow Networks, connect using HTTP first, and then connect using TCP/IP.

16. Select Basic Authentication under Proxy Authentication Settings.

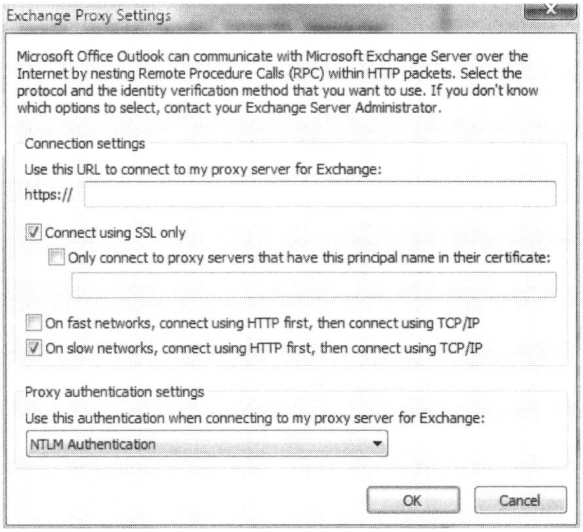

Figure 12-3. Configuring RPC over HTTP

17. Click OK twice, and then click Next.

18. Click Finish, and then click Close.

That was a long process, but you've finished configuring Outlook to use RPC over HTTP to connect to your Exchange Server machine. Now, simply open Outlook, and enter your credentials (format the username as *SHORTDOMAINNAME\ username*). You can choose to save the password. You'll then see your mailbox, and from then on, you won't see anything different than if you were directly connected to your corporate network in the office.

Using Cached Exchange Mode

Using Outlook 2007 in Cached Exchange Mode involves Outlook making a complete local copy of every item in your Exchange mailbox. Whether you are online or offline, you are always operating from that cache; Outlook synchronizes the local copy of your data with Exchange Server on a regular basis to keep both up-to-date. Incoming mail is directly pushed down to Outlook from Exchange Server if Outlook is directly connected to the same network as the server; otherwise, the client retrieves mail during a regular synchronization.

You can configure Cached Exchange Mode by clicking the Outlook icon in the bottom left of the window, as shown in Figure 12-4.

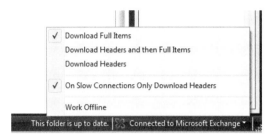

Figure 12-4. Configuring Cached Exchange Mode in Outlook 2007

Your options include the following:

Download Full Items: Selecting this option downloads all parts of messages, including headers, bodies, and attachments, when synchronization takes place.

Download Headers and Then Full Items: Selecting this option downloads just the headers of messages first and then downloads messages. This is useful on a slow connection where you want a quick survey of all the mail in your mailbox before downloading each individual item.

Download Headers: Selecting this option downloads only message headers, without the full bodies or any attachments.

On Slow Connections Only Download Headers: Outlook uses its internal logic to figure out whether you are on a particularly slow connection, and if it believes you are, it will download only headers.

Work Offline: Selecting this option cancels all synchronization and puts Outlook into offline mode. This is a toggle command; the check mark beside the item indicates its current state.

CHAPTER 13

Forms and Macros

So far you've seen just how versatile Outlook 2007 can be, and with a few tweaks here and there it's possible to do practically anything you need to do without having to get into complicated scripting or full-blown programming. Nevertheless, as with the rest of the Office suite, the underlying engine that powers Outlook is built on a highly versatile programming platform called Visual Basic for Applications (VBA), which allows virtually unlimited customization and programmatic manipulation of Outlook's functionality.

This chapter will introduce you to the concept of programmatically manipulating Outlook using two methods:

- Forms
- Macros

Forms, in their most general sense, are what you use every time you use Outlook. For example, a form can compile an email when you create a new contact item and when you add a new entry to the calendar. Microsoft has designed the forms you see and use every day based on commonly used tasks. We first will cover the set of standard forms delivered as part of Outlook, and then we will cover how to customize forms that don't quite deliver the functionality you need.

Understanding macros will take you to the next level of understanding Outlook (and the wider Office application development environment); with *macros*, you can automate tasks you perform regularly and augment Outlook functions with some of your own devising.

Understanding Outlook Forms

Every Outlook item is created from and based upon a form of some sort. For example, Outlook generates an email when you enter information into the standard message form, and in the same way, Outlook creates a contact when you enter contact information into the contact form.

The list of standard forms provided in Outlook is as follows:

- With the appointment form you can create and modify calendar entries.
- You can use the contact form to enter information about a person or an organization.
- With the distribution list form, you can address contacts as a single entity.
- You can use the journal form to create new Outlook journal entries.
- The meeting request form is a special form for creating and sending meeting requests that integrate into your calendar and allow recipients to respond.
- Use the message form to create and display email messages.
- Use the post form to allow threaded, bulletin-board style conversations to be displayed in a folder.
- The RSS article form is a new form that allows you to create a blog post directly from Outlook.
- The task form allows you to track a specific task that you need to address in a given time period.
- The task request form allows you to send tasks to remote users and allows them to respond accordingly.

You need to understand two more concepts before you can start customizing or creating your own forms: item types and message classes. *Item types* essentially allow you to programmatically access Outlook's inherent functionality, with types representing functionality such as email items, contact items, tasks, and appointments. These item types map quite nicely onto the standard forms list, and they provide the underlying capability that the form represents.

Message classes get further down into the weeds of Outlook and are the function calls used by Outlook when you use an item type through a form. In this way, if you use the contact form to add a new contact, from a user perspective you are using the ContactItem item type, and Outlook turns this into, programmatically, the IPM.Contact message class. If this sounds confusing, don't worry—it will become a little clearer as you continue through this chapter.

The best way to see how these aspects of form creation are linked together is to step through a working example. The following section covers how to customize an existing form in Outlook that is used for messaging.

Adding the BCC Field to the Message Form

As we've already said, Outlook comes with a set of standard forms you use in everyday Outlook activities, such as sending an email and adding a new contact. You can use these forms as templates for new forms, which allows you to customize the functionality based on existing Outlook capabilities. Take, for example, the email form used to create a standard email. With the standard form, you don't see the BCC field until you add a recipient to the BCC field in the Select Name: Contacts dialog box, shown in Figure 13-1.

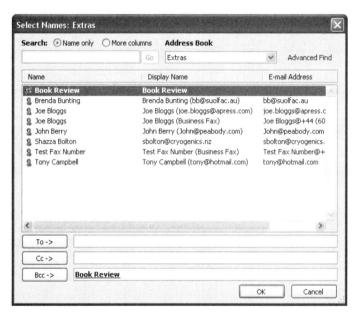

Figure 13-1. When you add a BCC contact to an email, the BCC field appears on the message form.

What we'll do now is show how to create a new form based on the standard messaging form that shows the BCC field by default. In this way, you can start typing in the BCC field automatically without having to click the To or CC button first.

The process for creating a new form based on the existing message form is as follows:

1. On the Tools menu, select Forms ➤ Design a Form to display the Design Form dialog box shown in Figure 13-2.

2. Make sure you are looking in the Standard Forms Library, then highlight Message, and finally click Open.

Figure 13-2. Select the form you want to use as your template.

3. Next, you'll see the form designer, where you can start to modify how the form looks. Notice, in Figure 13-3, the Field Chooser dialog box; you can use this dialog box to add fields to your form by dragging and dropping them in the location you want those fields represented on your form.

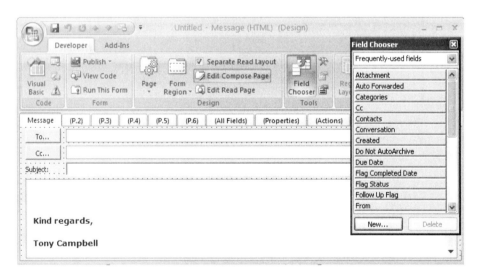

Figure 13-3. Use the Field Chooser dialog box to add new fields to your form design.

4. For this example, click the message body, and notice you can resize the whitespace used for the message. Use the topmost anchor to drag the window down far enough to leave space for the BCC field. Now, drag the Subject field down tight against the message body, as shown in Figure 13-4.

Figure 13-4. Resize the message body, and move the Subject field to make room for BCC.

5. In the Field Chooser dialog box, select Address Fields in the drop-down menu. You'll see the BCC field shown in the list, as per Figure 13-5.

Figure 13-5. Locate the BCC field in the Field Chooser dialog box.

6. Now, right-click BCC, drag it from the Field Chooser to the form designer, and drop it beneath CC. It should look something like Figure 13-6.

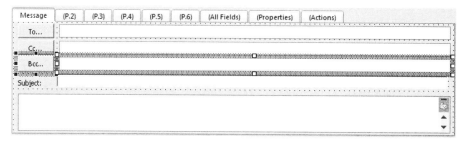

Figure 13-6. The BCC field should be neatly slotted between CC and Subject.

7. To change the look and feel of the BCC button, such as the font or type size, right-click the button, and select Properties. You can change the font to be the same as the other buttons by selecting Tahoma (see Figure 13-7).

Figure 13-7. Change the look and feel of the form using the Properties dialog box.

8. Once you are happy with the layout and spacing of your fields in the form, click the Publish button in the Form group on the Ribbon, and then select Publish Form.

9. In the Publish Form As dialog box, make sure you are looking in the Personal Forms Library, and then give the form a meaningful name, such as **BCCDefault**. Then click Publish.

10. You can now close your form designer; there is no need to save your work any further.

To use your newly created form, the next time you want to send an email with the BCC field already present on the screen when you start to generate the email, click Tools ➤ Form ➤ Choose a Form, and then look in the *Personal Forms Library*, select BCCDefault, and click Open. The BCC field will appear on the email message by default, as shown in Figure 13-8.

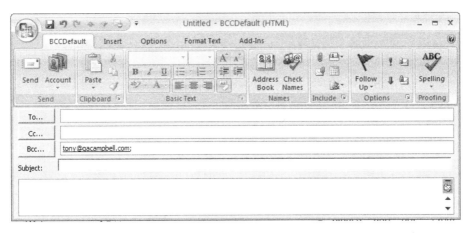

Figure 13-8. The BCC field now appears on all emails created using this form.

The amount of customization you do on a form can vary considerably from, as in the previous example, simply adding one extra field to the standard form template to completely customizing a form beyond all recognition to accomplish some specialized requirement for your own needs.

To make sure you create your form in a way that makes it as useful as possible, you need to completely understand your requirements before you start dabbling in the form designer. You also need to understand more than simply the fields you will be adding since the real strength of forms comes from how each field is handled when the form executes—for example, what happens when you click the Send button in the message form.

Using Controls

Controls are items on a form that allow you to manipulate some aspect of functionality, such as a scroll bar, checkbox, or radio button. You can add controls to a form by right-clicking anywhere on a blank space on your form (not to be confused with blank whitespace on the text part of the message) and selecting Control Toolbox. This will open the Toolbox shown in Figure 13-9.

Figure 13-9. The control Toolbox allows you to add user-based controls to a form.

To add a control to a form, simply drag the relevant control from the Toolbox and drop it on a blank part of the form. In each case, you can personalize the control by right-clicking it and selecting Properties. You can also modify the internal workings of the control through the Advanced Properties menu.

Building Forms with Custom Controls

A great feature of the Office suite is the tight integration across the application set. In this way, you can use other applications in Office 2007 as the basis for creating forms in Outlook. For example, if you wanted to create a form with embedded spreadsheet functionality that you could send as an email, you could create the form using an Excel spreadsheet and augment it with controls such as To, CC, and Subject to wrap it up as an email. The following procedure is the same for each Office application, but for this example we are using Excel:

1. Right-click anywhere on the Toolbox, and select Custom Controls. This opens the Additional Controls dialog box, shown in Figure 13-10.

2. Scroll down until you find Microsoft Office Spreadsheet 11.0, select it, and then click OK.

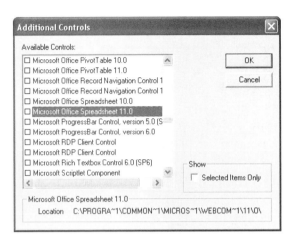

Figure 13-10. Add controls from other Office applications.

3. The Toolbox will now have the new spreadsheet control added at the bottom, as shown in Figure 13-11. You can add as many controls to your Toolbox as you desire.

Figure 13-11. You can add controls to the Toolbox for easy access.

4. Now, drag the spreadsheet to some blank space on your form, and size it accordingly, as shown in Figure 13-12.

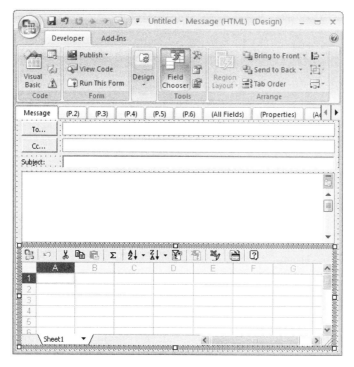

Figure 13-12. The spreadsheet control provides all the capabilities of Excel within Outlook.

5. When you're done, it's a matter of publishing the new form as you did previously.

When it comes to sending an email with this embedded spreadsheet, select Tools ➤ Forms ➤ Choose a Form, look in Personal Forms Library, and then select your new form. The email will look something like Figure 13-13.

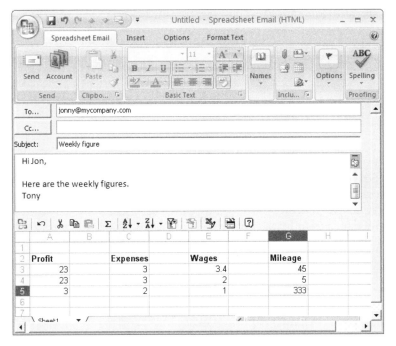

Figure 13-13. A new email containing an embedded spreadsheet

Sharing Forms with Other Users

You can share the forms you create with other users in two ways. You can publish the form (in the same way you published the BCC form earlier) to a public folder on an Exchange Server system, or you can save the file as an .oft file in a shared directory.

Since you've already used the publishing method (it's a matter of opening the folder list and locating your shared public folder), the following steps will explain how to share forms as .oft files:

1. In the form designer, instead of clicking the Publish button, click the Microsoft Office Button in the top-left corner, and then select Save As.

2. Locate the shared folder you want to store the .oft file in, give the file a meaningful name, and then click Save.

3. Close the form designer.

If another user wants to use the form you have saved, they should open Outlook, click File ➤ New ➤ Choose Form, and then select User Templates in File System in the Look In drop-down list. Next, navigate to the shared folder, then highlight the appropriate template, and finally click Open.

> **NOTE** Some custom templates may require you to lower your macro security settings to work properly. For more information about macro security, see Chapter 11.

Understanding Macros

A macro is a set of commands automatically executed in sequence. In Office terms, a macro is a small piece of VBA code that is used to control some aspect of how the Office application operates, and each Office application has its own integrated development environment (IDE) to allow you to write this code. VBA is a relatively easy programming language to learn, and the IDE certainly helps you generate bug-free code quickly by debugging code as you type. Nevertheless, if you want to learn more about VBA and developing complicated macros in Office, check out `http://msdn.` `microsoft.com`.

The following sections will show you the most basic example of a macro and how you can make it accessible in Outlook on the toolbar for immediate access.

Creating a Macro

To get started writing a macro, click Tools ➤ Macro ➤ Macros. You'll see the Macros dialog box. We'll start by showing how to create a macro that displays a greeting to the user. So, give the macro a name, such as **GreetingsFromOutlook**, as shown in Figure 13-14. Then click Create.

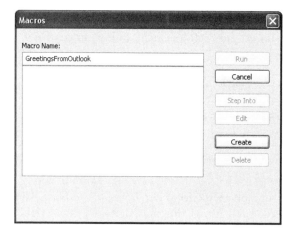

Figure 13-14. Naming the macro is the first step.

NOTE Macro names are used as function calls in the code and so cannot have spaces.

Now, you'll see the Microsoft Visual Basic IDE, as shown in Figure 13-15. Notice the macro name you created in the Macros dialog box has resulted in some code being added to the IDE.

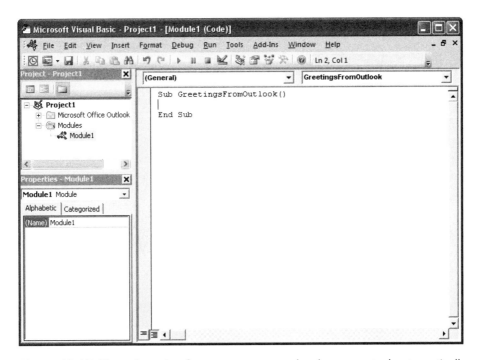

Figure 13-15. The subroutine for your new macro has been created automatically.

You'll see the cursor has automatically been placed between the Sub header and End Sub. Now, type the following line of code exactly as you see it here:

```
MsgBox ("Greetings From Outlook")
```

On the toolbar, immediately above where you typed the code, click the Play button (a little green arrow pointing to the right) to execute your code. The result will be a dialog box with your greeting inside, as shown in Figure 13-16. Click OK to return to the IDE.

Figure 13-16. Your macro displays a greeting in a dialog box, complete with the standard OK button.

To save your macro, click the File menu, and then select Save.

Running a Macro

You can execute a macro in a few ways once you've created it:

- Using the Macros dialog box
- Adding a macro to a toolbar

If you select Tools ➤ Macro ➤ Macros, you can highlight the macro of your choice in the list and click Run. This will execute your macro just like you previously executed it in the IDE.

Alternatively, you can add a macro to a toolbar by clicking View ➤ Toolbars ➤ Customize. Then in the Customize dialog box, focus on the Commands tab, and then highlight Macros on the list (shown in Figure 13-17).

Figure 13-17. Locate the macro in the Customize dialog box.

You'll see all the macros you have created in VBA listed on the Commands tab. Now, it's a simple matter of dragging the macro from the Commands tab to your toolbar where you can execute it with a single click, as shown in Figure 13-18.

Figure 13-18. The macro has been added to the standard Outlook toolbar.

Getting More Information About VBA

VBA programming is undoubtedly a huge subject, and it would be foolish of us to try to cover it in detail in this book; however, now that we've whetted your appetite for macros, here are three of what we consider to be the best resources on the Internet for learning about VBA:

- The first place to start with any research into Office 2007 and VBA is Microsoft's very own developer website: `http://msdn.microsoft.com`.
- A fellow Apress author, Rod Stephens, runs an extremely popular site devoted to all things Visual Basic: `http://www.vb-helper.com`.
- There are a variety of tricks, tips, and forums for asking questions of other developers at this site: `http://www/outlookcode.com/d/`.

Index

H

FIND IT FAST
with the Apress *SuperIndex*™

Quickly Find Out What the Experts Know

Leading by innovation, Apress now offers you its *SuperIndex*™, a turbocharged companion to the fine index in this book. The Apress *SuperIndex*™ is a keyword and phrase-enabled search tool that lets you search through the entire Apress library. Powered by dtSearch™, it delivers results instantly.

Instead of paging through a book or a PDF, you can electronically access the topic of your choice from a vast array of Apress titles. The Apress *SuperIndex*™ is the perfect tool to find critical snippets of code or an obscure reference. The Apress *SuperIndex*™ enables all users to harness essential information and data from the best minds in technology.

No registration is required, and the Apress *SuperIndex*™ is free to use.

❶ Thorough and comprehensive searches of over 300 titles

❷ No registration required

❸ Instantaneous results

❹ A single destination to find what you need

❺ Engineered for speed and accuracy

❻ Will spare your time, application, and anxiety level

Search now: *http://superindex.apress.com*

You Need the Companion eBook

Your purchase of this book entitles you to buy the companion PDF-version eBook for only $10. Take the weightless companion with you anywhere.

We believe this Apress title will prove so indispensable that you'll want to carry it with you everywhere, which is why we are offering the companion eBook (in PDF format) for $10 to customers who purchase this book now. Convenient and fully searchable, the PDF version of any content-rich, page-heavy Apress book makes a valuable addition to your programming library. You can easily find and copy code—or perform examples by quickly toggling between instructions and the application. Even simultaneously tackling a donut, diet soda, and complex code becomes simplified with hands-free eBooks!

Once you purchase your book, getting the $10 companion eBook is simple:

❶ Visit **www.apress.com/promo/tendollars/**.

❷ Complete a basic registration form to receive a randomly generated question about this title.

❸ Answer the question correctly in 60 seconds, and you will receive a promotional code to redeem for the $10.00 eBook.

2560 Ninth Street • Suite 219 • Berkeley, CA 94710

eBookshop

THE EXPERT'S VOICE™

Offer valid through 9/07.